The Pastor's

HOSPITAL MINISTRY

The Pastor's
HOSPITAL MINISTRY

Richard K. Young

BROADMAN PRESS
NASHVILLE, TENNESSEE

Printed in the United States of America
1.5O59KSP

Lovingly Dedicated

to

POLLY
and our
VICKI *and* DICK

FOREWORD

I

"Man needs religion and particularly when he is sick"
—Henry A. Christian, M.D.

Of all professional men, the pastor and the family doctor
need to work most closely together. The same word can
be used to describe the daily work of each. *Webster's New
International Dictionary* defines the verb "minister" as "to
do things needful or helpful; to attend and serve; to perform service in any office, sacred or secular." Certainly
proper concern for the welfare of the human beings under
their care should make the physician and the pastor eager
to work together for their good. Often each could contribute effectively to the other's efforts to help someone who
is sick in body, mind, and soul. The importance of what
has been aptly called "the comprehensive approach" to the
patient was recognized twenty-four centuries ago by Plato,
but was almost forgotten until comparatively recent times.
With the increasing recognition of the effect which the
emotions have upon the bodily functions (psychosomatic
medicine), more and more pastors and doctors are learning
that they can be mutually helpful in their common field
of service to the sick person.

The concept of the physician and pastor as members of a

team devoted to healing is gaining ground. One of the most thoughtful and dynamic leaders in this field is the author of this book. Since 1946 he has been chaplain of the North Carolina Baptist Hospital, and he has both learned and taught a great deal in that time. This book, the result of his work as counselor, teacher, and earnest seeker for truth, is a noteworthy contribution to the subject. It represents the result of much hard work and concentrated thinking, and should be stimulating and helpful to all who are concerned with the welfare of the people to whom they minister, either as pastor or as physician.

WINGATE M. JOHNSON, M.D.
Chief of Staff, Private Diagnostic Clinic, Bowman Gray School of Medicine of Wake Forest College

II

In the field of psychiatry there has been a decided trend, since World War I, toward more and more co-operation and correlation with professions that are concerned with human relations and problems of adjustment.

Child guidance clinics brought about a working team composed of psychiatrists, social workers, and psychologists. Before long a closer liaison with pediatricians was established, and then anthropologists, educators, ministers, and nurses came into the team along with other doctors in the large field of psychosomatic medicine.

The preceding paragraph was written from a strictly psychiatric point of view, as is readily observable. A very similar paragraph could be written by a minister, a nurse, or others, showing an analogous trend of development. Without going further back into history, it can be recorded that early in the 1920's when child guidance clinics began to flourish, ministers, psychiatrists, and other doctors were getting together in seminars, courses, and even in clinical teamwork. As an example, the developments in Boston and Worcester may be cited. Dr. Cabot's book *What Men Live By* illustrates a medical point of view at that time.

In this business of teamwork that is designed to help other people, we must have on the part of the helper a greater breadth of knowledge, enhanced skill in "techniques," and more empathy. Of course, doctors cannot be ministers or lawyers, nor can ministers be psychiatrists or social workers in the full sense of these professional delineations. No one should pretend to be versed in the knowledge and skills of more than one or two professions. In other words, we must work together.

From another point of view, attention is called to the fact that almost one half of the patients coming into the general practitioner's office may not have a physical disorder as the primary cause of symptoms. The cause may be found in conflict, emotional upheaval, and immaturity. Ordinarily, the general practitioner does not have ready access to a psychiatrist or a skilled psychiatric social worker. However, the chances are very good that a minister knows the patient or the patient's family and, of course, is ready to help. This throws an additional challenge to the minister, and this book should be very helpful to him in fulfilling his role.

Knowing Dr. Young personally and having worked with him in many instances, it is my opinion that he is presenting here an up-to-date factual treatise and guide as well as a down-to-earth philosophy that should serve well all of us who are trying to help our fellow man find the way toward health and happiness.

LLOYD J. THOMPSON, M.D.
Professor and Chairman of the Department of Psychiatry, Bowman Gray School of Medicine of Wake Forest College

CONTENTS

INTRODUCTION

The care of the sick has in this decade grown into a matter of national interest and public policy. In the seven-year period from 1946 to 1952, nearly four hundred new hospitals were completed and put to use in the United States. The Hill-Burton Act is expected to double the number of community-serving general hospitals in this country. Approximately 100,000,000 persons in this country have some form of hospitalization insurance. The number of hospital admissions for the nation increased from 15,500,000 in 1946 to 19,500,000 in 1952.

The trend is definitely established. The doctor practices medicine largely today in his office or in the local hospital. No one would deny that the pastor performs an increasing portion of his ministry to sick people in the same local hospitals.

Much has been said in recent years in the field of pastoral care about closer co-operation between the minister and the doctor. Yet church-related hospitals have been slow to furnish the leadership and make available to pastors and theological students their clinical facilities where they could train alongside the medical interns. More pastors feel inadequate in their hospital ministry than in any other phase of the pastoral office.

Many of the ideas in this book have been expressed in one way or another in the current literature on pastoral care. The trained hospital chaplain experiences every day the tremendous advantages that accrue from co-operation with the medical profession, but no one thus far has correlated the chaplain's findings with the express purpose of helping a pastor to become a member of the healing team in his local hospital.

For example, as this is being written there are twelve North Carolina pastors at the Baptist Hospital for a period of six weeks, mingling with seventy-five interns, assistant residents, and resident doctors, as the pastor and the doctor, each in his own role, minister to the same patient. The "comprehensive approach" to medicine is the door and the local hospital is the stage upon which the sick people in our society can become the recipients of a more vital ministry than either the doctor or the minister can offer separately.

As the "know-how" of co-operation is gained in the teaching institution, the doctor and the minister can carry to the local community the same benefits for the total welfare of the people to whom they are responsible. Just as the doctor makes his daily visit to his local hospital the pastor likewise visits his church members who are sick and in the hospital. Instead of a bare acquaintance in many instances, and hostility in some cases, there should exist between these two most influential members of the community the strongest bond of mutual endeavor and oneness of purpose: the wholeness of man in body, mind, and spirit.

I am convinced that medical education at the present time is more advanced than theological education in preparing its students to co-operate with other professions in the ministry of healing. Furthermore, from my observation, the failures of the minister that have irritated the doctor, for the most part, have been very simple and unintentional mistakes which stem from a lack of knowledge of how to work in the hospital environment. It should, therefore, be emphasized that the minister cannot, outside the hospital environment, experience a dynamic learning relationship of functioning as a member of a healing team.

I have had two objectives in mind while writing this book. One is to stimulate interest in the field of pastoral care in order that more facilities may be provided for training purposes and, consequently, more emphasis placed upon the healing ministry of the pastor. The second objective is to present to the pastor, as practically as possible, some suggestions for improving his skill in the care of souls as he works in his own local hospital.

The ideas expressed in this book have been wrought out and tested during the seven-year period that I have spent as chaplain in a medical center. The members of the medical and nursing professions with whom I have worked in this environment have taught me a great deal. Dr. Wingate Johnson, Dr. Angus Randolph, and Dr. Manson Meads, members of the faculty of the Bowman Gray School of Medicine, particularly merit my sincere appreciation for what they have taught me about the art of ministering to people.

Further words of appreciation are due many people who have helped in the preparation of this book. A part of this material was presented in my doctoral thesis to the Southern Baptist Theological Seminary.

Dr. Olin T. Binkley of the Southeastern Baptist Theological Seminary, in spite of a crowded schedule, was kind enough to read the manuscript in its entirety and to offer wise counsel and encouragement.

Several individuals who were participating in our clinical training program while this work was in progress were especially helpful: Elmer West, Robert Whiteside, Harry McCartney, Bill Bassett, Bob Dorr, Dean Bergen, Gene Floyd, and Arnold Smith.

I am sincerely grateful to Mrs. Marjorie Northup, my secretary, for typing this material, and to Mrs. Catherine Jackson for her editorial help. To my wife I am grateful for her patience, which carried over to Vicki and Dick, who, though young in years, were very much aware that these pages were being written.

RICHARD K. YOUNG

North Carolina Baptist Hospital
Winston-Salem, North Carolina

The Pastor's

HOSPITAL MINISTRY

Chapter One

THE HEALING TEAM

Mr. A. is forty-three years of age and has suffered from recurring attacks of ulcerative colitis for more than twelve months. During his second hospitalization period a psychiatrist and a chaplain were called in on Mr. A.'s case. He talked at length with the psychiatrist about his divorce which took place two years previous to his illness and also about pressures related to his vocation. Following Mr. A.'s interview with the psychiatrist the chaplain entered the picture. After introducing himself as the minister who worked full-time with the patients in the hospital, Mr. A. immediately responded, "Preacher, I want to talk to you." The information which followed revealed a recent affair with a married woman and the fact that Mr A. was confronted by the husband the day before he was brought to the hospital with a severe attack of ulcerative colitis. Six months have passed and Mr. A.'s condition has not required further medical attention.

This generation has seen medical science pass through a period of extreme specialization. The total human organism has been broken down and its minute parts studied intently, so that now there is a specialist for practically every organ of the human body. Because of the increased knowledge which resulted from this approach, the life expectancy at birth is seventeen years longer than it was at the beginning of this century. Nevertheless, many baffling problems were encountered by these medical specialists because they forgot to consider the patient as a whole person. Attention was focused upon the diseased organ to the exclusion of the sick patient.

Many centuries ago, Plato had recognized the pitfalls of this type of medical practice, and pointed them out in *Charmides:*

As you ought not to attempt to cure the eyes without the head, or the head without the body, so neither ought you to attempt to cure the body without the soul; and this . . . is the reason why the cure of many diseases is unknown to the physicians of Hellas, because they are ignorant of the whole, which ought to be studied also; for the part can never be well unless the whole is well. . . . And therefore, if the head and body are to be well, you must begin by curing the soul; that is the first thing.[1]

A contemporary authority on the mind-body relationship, Dr. Flanders Dunbar, has written:

The belief that the patient should be treated as a whole goes back beyond anything most of us would consider as medicine at all. The witch doctor of our primitive ancestors was both physician and priest. He worked on the patient's psychic trouble as on his bodily symptoms, for he never knew there was any real difference between them. In fact, the witch doctor's cures were probably due as much to his treatment of the emotions as to his herbs or bloodletting.[2]

That mind affects body and body affects mind are scientific facts. One has only to strap a dog down on a laboratory table, place a fluoroscope over his stomach, and shake a cat in his face to see how anger affects the digestive apparatus. Recently a doctor stopped me in the hospital and asked if I had been in Room 221. When I replied that I

---

[1] Plato, "Charmides," *The Dialogues of Plato,* translated by B. Jowett (New York: Random House, 1937), v.

[2] Flanders Dunbar, M.D., *Mind and Body: Psychosomatic Medicine* (New York: Random House, 1947), pp. vii, viii.

had, he asked, "What happened while you were in the room?" I told him that the patient had gone through a long, distorted confession which involved bitterness and hatred toward a fellow member of his church. The doctor responded, "I knew something had happened; the patient's blood pressure has gone down."

Every person has a reaction pattern in life all his own. The same incidents that arouse anger and fear in one individual may have no effect at all on another. One's reaction pattern, or "way of life," either contributes toward health or tends to foster sickness. Kraines and Thetford have described what happens to the functions (physiology) of the human body when the sympathetic portion of the autonomic nervous system is stimulated:

The blood pressure is increased, the heart beats faster, the blood vessels contract, the stomach dilates, the gastric secretion tends to diminish, the intestines relax, the heat regulation is changed so that more heat is lost, the adrenal glands are stimulated, the liver secretes more glycogen which changes to blood sugar, the blood clots more easily: in other words, the sympathetic nervous system automatically increases the activity of every organ, prepares the total organism to meet the immediate situation. The reverse situation obtains when the organism is resting: the parasympathetic system automatically slows down the activity of each organ.[3]

Slang expressions used to describe states of fear or anger —"worried sick," "so mad I could pop," "blind with rage," "trembling like a leaf," "burned up," "letting off steam," to give a few examples—come surprisingly close to describing what actually happens to the physical body as a result of strong emotion.

Psychology and psychiatry have played an important role in the mind-body (psychosomatic) concept that has come to

[3] S. H. Kraines and E. S. Thetford, *Managing Your Mind* (New York: The Macmillan Company, 1943), p. 20.

influence medical practice, and in many instances specialists in these fields have collaborated with the physiologist
to solve various clinical problems.

In his threefold ministry of preaching, teaching, and
healing, Jesus recognized the essential unity of man's nature. He did not treat the individual primarily as a body
or as a soul, but ministered to the whole person, placing
emphasis upon the totality of body, mind, and spirit. The
text of his first sermon indicates that the relief of human
suffering was a primary purpose of his mission:

> The spirit of the Lord is upon me: for he has consecrated
> me to preach the gospel to the poor, he has sent me to pro-
> claim release for the captives and recovery of sight for the
> blind, to set free the oppressed.[4]

Jesus' concern for people, the fact that he cared for the
individual, is evident in every personal encounter. It might
be a well-known official who came at midnight, a woman
taken in adultery, a leper crying for mercy, a madman
among the tombs, or a bereaved family—regardless of the
circumstances, Jesus was sensitive to the need and wanted
to help.

The knowledge that God cares for each of us and that
he is always ready to forgive can be a potent factor in the
healing of disease in man's body as well as in his soul. A
woman in a four-bed ward spoke up one day and said,
"Chaplain, step over here a minute. I would like to tell
you about my 'new found joy.'" She continued, "Last
night as I lay here fretting over my condition, I decided
to place my life in the hands of God as I had never done
before. Then it was that I experienced what I am calling
my 'new found joy.' I cannot even believe that with my
type of personality I am lying here facing the greatest difficulty of my life, yet conscious of a peace that is indescrib-

---

[4] Luke 4:18 Moffatt.

able." This woman had a blood clot in one of her veins that the doctors were attempting to dissolve before it reached her heart, and she was aware of this fact. Certainly the peace which had come to her as a result of her surrender to God was an asset to the doctors in their battle with her physical disease.

Jesus commissioned his followers to preach the gospel and to heal the sick. In the early church the ministry of healing was vital, as well as the ministry of the Word. Yet Christians since the days of the apostles have had to look back with wistful longing, hoping for the day when religion would again be closely related to healing as such. The opportunity which exists in this generation to enter into a total ministry to the total person is the greatest which the church has faced since Jesus set the example.

However, the need must be seen before the job can be done. In the past the church has not only failed to see the need, but has actually opposed the progress of medical science. In A.D. 529 Emperor Justinian, acting upon the advice of church dignitaries, closed the medical schools of Athens and Alexandria. In 1215 Pope Innocent III condemned surgery and all priests who practiced it. In 1248 the dissection of the human body was pronounced sacrilegious, and the study of anatomy was banned.[5] Thus began a breach between the church and medicine which has continued to this generation. This breach has perhaps been widened by Christian Science, which emphasizes the ministry of healing but divorces itself completely from medical science.

Today medical science is pointing out the need for a total approach to the total person and is teaching the wholeness of personality. In the light of this fact, is not the church obligated to re-emphasize its ministry of healing

---

[5] George Gordon Dawson, *Healing: Pagan and Christian* (London: The Society for Promoting Christian Knowledge, 1935), pp. 172–174.

and to prepare its pastors for more intelligent co-operation with the medical profession? No one can deny that this complex society in which we live is producing many sick and confused people whose souls are as much in need of healing as their bodies. The need for a ministry of healing on the part of the church is illustrated by the following facts:

1. Two famous medical authorities, Weiss and English, say that one third of all the patients who consult physicians today do not have any definite bodily disease to account for their symptoms. In another third, emotional factors are contributing to the disability produced by organic disease.[6]

2. Sales of books and magazines directed toward the troubled soul in this land are enormous. Literature on the subjects of nervousness, tension, guilt, anxiety, frustration, peace, and happiness is gobbled up by readers today in wholesale quantities. *Peace of Mind* by Joshua Liebman led the list of best-sellers in this country for nearly twelve months. This record is indicative of a hunger in society that cannot be denied.

3. There are only about fifty-five hundred practicing psychiatrists in the United States, and most of these are concentrated in medical centers or large cities. Dr. Douglas Kelley, formerly associate professor of psychiatry at the Bowman Gray School of Medicine in Winston-Salem, North Carolina, said in a speech to theological students:

The minister occupies a unique role in society. Because of the very nature of his work he is called in when the burdens of a family are unbearable, thus having the opportunity in many instances to uncover psychiatric disease which would otherwise develop into an incurable state. If he is aware of this condition and can recognize early mental disorder, he can render a signal service to the community.

---

[6] Edward Weiss, M.D., and O. Spurgeon English, M.D., *Psychosomatic Medicine* (Philadelphia: W. B. Saunders Co., 1949) pp. 1–2.

4. Very few cities in the South have escaped the faith-healing tent in recent years. One such tent, put up on the edge of Winston-Salem in the summer of 1952 was said to seat five thousand people. Several transfer trucks were connected with the outfit; altogether a hundred thousand dollars must have been invested in the equipment. People came to this tent by ambulance from distances as great as forty miles.

So-called "faith-healers" are a thorny problem to the pastor and the hospital chaplain. One such man entered a certain prominent hospital during the visiting hours, bringing a bottle of olive oil. He visited a thirty-three-year-old woman, a deaf-mute, who was recuperating from an eye operation, and who was not supposed to wash her face or comb her hair for two weeks after the operation. The faith-healer pulled back the bandages from the patient's eye and swabbed her face with olive oil, rupturing several blood vessels in the eye. Intelligent ministers who are seeking a better relationship with the medical profession should keep in mind that most doctors have had unpleasant experiences at one time or another with such overzealous religious enthusiasts.

5. More and more medical practitioners today are eager for the church to help them by ministering to the spiritual needs of the emotionally sick patients who are crowding their offices. They are recognizing the relationship of body and spirit; and they welcome sound help. A leading surgeon said to me recently, "I am a surgeon. I stayed in my office yesterday from five o'clock until six talking to a man about what was more of a spiritual problem than a surgical one, and I am not adequately trained for that kind of task." He further stated, "If I had my life to live over, I would prepare myself to deal with the mass of people in society today that are being brushed off by the doctor and are not being helped by the church."

This new emphasis in medicine and the greater opportunities now open to the church in the field of healing are not without pitfalls. When trends of thought in any field begin to shift, the pendulum tends to swing to the limit before finding its true center. This is especially true when an idea becomes popularized and a certain amount of glamor is attached to it. Psychiatry has had to face this problem since World War II. Nowadays the word "psychosomatic" can be rolled off the tongue by the novice as expertly as the word "Mesopotamia."

Doctors have been caught in this shift of thinking in regard to the diagnostic approach to the patient and now have to guard against the danger of overlooking real organic trouble in patients who are obviously neurotic. Dr. Wingate Johnson, chief of the Private Diagnostic Clinic of the Bowman Gray School of Medicine, relates an experience that taught him a lesson at the time when he began to recognize the importance of emotional factors in illness. A young man had reacted to a notice from his draft board by developing many symptoms referred to his digestive system. After consulting Dr. Johnson several times in his office, the young man sent for him to come to his boarding house because he thought he had appendicitis. Resisting a natural impulse to give the patient a figurative "kick in the pants," the doctor examined him and found that, in spite of every effort to divert his attention, the muscles remained rigid over the appendix area. When some fever was found, a white blood cell count was made and found to be elevated. The young man was sent to the hospital, where the surgeon removed an acutely inflamed appendix.

Dr. Johnson commented that while the doctor's, or the patient's, guardian angel may have averted a ruptured appendix in this case, unnecessary operations are performed only too often for conditions resulting from emotional upsets. "Too many medical materialists do not recognize the very important part that the emotions play in their patients' symptoms, and have neither the time nor the patience to search for such factors."

Analogous to the physician who has "gone overboard" on the subject of psychosomatic medicine is the pastor who has had a little learning in the field of pastoral care and has become enamored of psychological concepts. Congregations have complained of having felt analyzed after his Sunday morning sermon. Such a minister is in danger of allowing basic theological beliefs to fade into the background, and of presenting Christianity on the level of how to keep an office force happy and how to be successful in business.

At the other extreme is the minister who blandly reiterates, "Jesus is the answer," and refuses to search for truth wherever manifestations of truth may be found. The accumulated knowledge of personality development garnered by scientific methods in recent years, coupled with a genuine love for people, can become a golden key in the hands of the minister to open doors in the lives of people through which Christ may enter. Then it is that Christianity permeates the total personality and influences every interpersonal relationship. Thus the "good news" that "Jesus is the answer" rises above the realm of meaningless "marketplace phrases" (as Sir Francis Bacon put it), and becomes a dynamic force for good in the personality of the individual. It is useless to try to force a truth—even the greatest of truths—willy-nilly upon every individual regardless of *how* and *why* Christ is the answer for his particular personality.

The minister and the doctor have more or less gone their separate ways in the past, with few attempts toward co-operation on either side. Today the hospital chaplain and doctor in the general hospital are finding that co-operation is extremely advantageous to the patient. Medical schools today are beginning to teach what is called the "comprehensive approach" to the patient. The following case history [7] will illustrate this method of approach:

A 27-year-old married housewife was admitted to the North Carolina Baptist Hospital on July 11, 1952, with the diagnosis of poliomyelitis. The patient was 6½ months pregnant at the time. She had been perfectly well until three days before admission, when she began to have severe headache and vomiting. On the day prior to admission marked weakness developed in the right leg. Physical examination on admission showed an apprehensive patient with fever, a viable uterine pregnancy, and a segmental type of paralysis involving several muscle groups in the right leg. During the next 48 hours this paralysis progressed to involve the entire right leg, then the entire left leg and bladder, with weakness of the abdominal and back muscles. Laboratory examinations confirmed the clinical impression of poliomyelitis.

Social and economic history: The patient was the only child of rather elderly parents. She had a severe attack of scarlet fever in childhood, and was kept in bed for approximately two months. The parents were financially well to do, and were oversolicitous of this child. She was more strongly attached to her mother than to her father. At the age of 21 she married a man who was four years her senior. They had one child, aged 3, living and well. The husband was in good health and owned an interest in a garage and an automobile agency. The marriage has apparently been quite happy except for tension between the husband and the patient's mother, apparently

---

[7] Prepared by Dr. Manson Meads, Head of the Department of Preventive Medicine at the Bowman Gray School of Medicine, Winston-Salem, North Carolina.

based on the mother's oversolicitous attitude toward her daughter.

The family lived in a rented home and was making plans just prior to the patient's illness to obtain a GI loan and build a small home of their own. They owned their own car, and the family income amounted to approximately $5,000 per year. The husband had carried poliomyelitis insurance (maximum coverage of $9,000) for two years, but when the patient came into the hospital there was some question as to whether this policy had been renewed before the onset of the patient's illness. (Note: In November, 1952—five months after the onset of the illness—it was decided by the insurance company that the policy was in force when the patient's illness began.)

Emotional status of the patient: On admission the patient was extremely apprehensive. She was aware that the diagnosis of poliomyelitis had been entertained by her family physician. She had little information regarding the nature of the disease, but her predominant fear was for the welfare of the child *in utero.* Prior to her illness the patient was apparently fairly well adjusted emotionally. She had a high school education.

Emotional reaction of the family: The husband demonstrated the expected anxiety regarding his wife, but was co-operative and understanding. The patient's father took a similar attitude. The mother was extremely upset, became overindulgent and unco-operative, and disturbed both the patient and the medical and nursing personnel. She disregarded hospital visiting hours and was a definite problem for the first several weeks of the patient's hospital stay.

Therapy of the acute phase of the illness

1. For the patient
   a. Physical factors: Absolute bed rest, position-
      ing in bed, hot packs for relief of muscle
      spasm, treatment of bladder paralysis, pre-
      vention of bladder infection.
   b. Emotional factors: Use of sedatives, reas-
      surance of the patient that her disease would
      not affect her child *in utero,* simple explana-
      tions regarding the disease and assurance that
      the great majority of individuals recover
      without any permanent disability.
2. For the family: An attempt was made to see the
   family before they saw the patient. At this time
   they were given a simple explanation of the
   disease, told that it was impossible to predict
   the outcome of the disease during the acute
   phase, and reassured as to the general prognosis
   in poliomyelitis. The family was particularly instructed to present a cheerful and confident appearance at the patient's bedside.

*Essential members of the therapeutic team during
the acute phase:* The internist (medical doctor), the
urologist, the nurse, the chaplain, the physiotherapist,
and the obstetrician.

Course in the hospital: The patient had no fever
after her fourth day in the hospital. The paralysis of
the bladder was transient and passed off in a period
of two weeks. Paralysis did not progress further, and
she had none of the dangerous complications associated with the bulbar form of this disease. During
the first three weeks of this patient's hospital stay
she was quite unstable emotionally. She had daily
periods of depression with crying spells, did little to
help herself, and called on her special nurses for the

most minor services. It was felt that her mother
played a large part in maintaining this attitude of
dependency. Her pregnancy added considerably to
her discomfort at bedrest. The chaplain's daily visits
did much to encourage the patient and her family.
It was largely through his efforts that the parents
acquired a more normal attitude, which greatly
helped the patient to become adjusted to her chronic
illness.

Therapeutic approach to early convalescence

1. For the patient
   a. Physical factors: Limited physiotherapy and
      maintenance of nutrition.
   b. Emotional factors: Reassurance and aid in
      the patient's adjustment to long-term con-
      valescence. Psychological preparation of the
      patient for transfer to a convalescent home
      specifically adapted to the treatment of polio-
      myelitis.
2. For the family: Further explanation as to the
   prognosis in this case (very probable residual
   paralysis for life). Encouragement in going
   ahead with plans for a small home adapted to a
   handicapped person. Reassurance regarding economic factors. (Contact was made with the local
   chapter of the National Foundation for Infantile
   Paralysis, which assured the family that the
   costs of this illness would be borne by that organization if the private insurance policy was
   found to be void.)

   One important phase in preparing for the
   transfer of the patient from this hospital to the
   convalescent center was a trip by the husband,
   the father, and the physician in charge to the
   convalescent home. At this time the members of

the family were reassured by what they saw and by the excellent facilities available. This trip greatly aided the patient in making the transition from the closely supervised existence of a general hospital to the group supervision which is necessary and important in a convalescent home.

Members of the therapeutic team during the convalescence: The internist, the orthopedist, the physiotherapist, the nurse, the hospital chaplain, the obstetrician, and the poliomyelitis foundation.

Subsequent course: After four weeks in the North Carolina Baptist Hospital the patient was transferred to a poliomyelitis center. Prior to her discharge, arrangements were made for a competent internist to assume the direct responsibility for the patient, and for a competent obstetrician to take over the obstetrical aspects of this case. Reports four months after the patient's discharge from the North Carolina Baptist Hospital indicate that the patient is doing well but will have permanent paralysis of both lower limbs. Two months after discharge the patient was delivered of a normal child.

This "comprehensive approach" being taught in progressive medical schools today has tremendous significance for the church and for its future ministry of healing. The church-related hospital is afforded an opportunity to offer a more distinctively Christian ministry than was conceived of when many of these hospitals were founded. When denominations first became interested in establishing hospitals, these institutions were badly needed by society. Today, however, the government is seeking to provide better medical care for its citizens, and through the Medical Care Commission money has been made available for building hospitals throughout the country. Yet even be-fore Congress took this action, many church-related hos-pitals, like some colleges and universities founded by religious impetus, had strayed far afield from the distinc-tive purpose envisioned by their founding fathers.

Today church-related hospitals must make their min-istry of healing distinctive in order to justify their exist-ence. Rethinking the purpose of these institutions in present-day society may return them closer to the original ideas promulgated by the founders of these institutions. For example, five motives for the hospital ministry of Southern Baptists can be stated: (1) to give medical care to the poor, (2) to carry out the healing ministry of Jesus, (3) to provide a Christian atmosphere for the sick, (4) to train godly young women in the field of nursing and to furnish an avenue of service to doctors and nurses who feel the Christian call, (5) to enlarge its program of evange-lism.

Space does not permit a detailed answer to the question, "What, then, is the function of these Baptist hospitals to-day in the light of the purposes for which they were founded?" Suffice it to say that in 1950 the denomination gave 48 cents per patient per day for the charity work of these hospitals. Some states supported their hospitals more generously than others, and some hospitals accomplished more than others with available funds for charity patients and other phases of hospital work as a Christian ministry. In 1950 seventeen of the Baptist hospitals in the South did not have departments of religion and only fifteen had hospital chaplains—one on a part-time basis. Of the fif-teen chaplains, only five had received specialized training for this work. At this writing only three hospitals have made any effort to set up a clinical training program in pastoral care for ministers.

In a speech made to the Southern Baptist Hospital Administrators at their convention in 1950, J. F. Murrell, administrator of the Miami Baptist Hospital in Oklahoma, said:

Baptists will use their hospitals to greater spiritual ends when they institute a program for training men for the highly specialized task of ministering to the sick. Theological training, as furnished by our seminaries, is essential as a background, but it is not enough. A clinical training program for this work is vitally needed, for only when we have men especially trained for this task will they fit into the hospital routine and be welcomed by the physicians and nurses, because they work along sound lines and co-operate with them and do not work independently of them.

It is imperative that denominational hospitals have chaplains trained to work with the medical profession. These medical facilities must now be made available to the seminary student, and this clinical training in pastoral care must be recognized as a definite part of his theological education.

In the light of the demands that have already arisen, Southern Baptists are several years behind the need in offering hospital facilities for clinical pastoral training to seminary students and pastors. The North Carolina Baptist Hospital has had more than 100 ministers from seventeen states enrolled in its training program within the past six years. At the present time it is receiving more than five times as many applications as it can accommodate. A recent three-day Institute on Pastoral Care drew more than 350 ministers from seven different states. This large enrolment is indicative of a hunger on the part of the minister for more skill to deal with the problems produced by this complex society. Hospitals and seminaries should satisfy this hunger.

The "comprehensive approach" in medical education today is significant not only to the church-related hospital but to the local church and the ministry of the local pastor as well. Medical students who are being taught to consider the social, economic, physiological, psychological, and spiritual factors in the diagnosis and treatment of the patient and who are learning to co-operate with the nurse, the social worker, the psychiatrist, the psychologist, and the chaplain in the hospital setting are going back into the local communities to practice. The tremendous need for spiritual healing which exists in society today, as well as the vast amount of scientific knowledge now available for a better understanding of the human personality, has been pointed out earlier in this chapter. These facts offer convincing evidence that the church, and more specifically the minister, should be engaged in a larger healing ministry than is being offered by most churches today.

We have too long thought of Jesus' threefold ministry as three functions which were practiced separately. Healing, being the most difficult to understand, has been relegated by the church almost entirely to institutions set up for that purpose and turned over to the exclusive use of the medical profession.

Before any suggestions for enlarging the healing ministry of the church can be considered, one must face the undeniable fact that the pastor of the average sized church already has his hands more than full. Sermon preparation, administrative duties, the educational program of the church, congregational crises, and family responsibilities leave little time for a counseling ministry. Yet the needs of the individual must not be overlooked if we are to follow the example of Jesus. Time after time he singled the individual out from the masses and dealt with persons one by one. Often the multitude received their lesson as Jesus ministered to an individual in their midst. An apparently disproportionate amount of his time was given to a small group of men, but these men were largely responsible for the spread of the gospel after his death. Perhaps the time-consuming task encountered in the individual ministry is filled with more potentialities than has been realized.

A few suggestions for enlarging the healing ministry of the church may be offered here. The first eight points are applicable principally to the local church and its pastor.

1. The young man entering the ministry today should be equipped to recognize early mental and emotional disorders. It has been said that one of every twelve babies born in this country will need psychiatric help before he dies. The minister who learns to recognize psychiatric problems and to aid these people in finding the help they need will have few bitter experiences like that of a pastor who recently drove more than 200 miles to my office and was on the verge of a nervous breakdown when I saw him. He had been asked to resign his church because a woman had spread false rumors in the community about his character. The woman was later examined and found to be mentally sick. The knowledge of a few simple facts concerning the "paranoid" type of mental illness would have enabled this pastor to recognize the woman's condition and probably to have avoided this tragedy.

2. The pastor should obtain the necessary training required to work skilfully with other professional people in the community, and should remember that they, too, in many instances are consecrated to the service of humanity with a deep sense of mission in their profession.

3. Immediately upon arriving in his pastorate the minister should learn about the various community service agencies which are available to people in need and should become acquainted with the key people connected with them.

4. Every minister should have a good working relationship with the doctors in his community. Three years ago a

minister in North Carolina was urged by a doctor on his board of deacons to take a ten weeks' course in clinical pastoral training at a medical center. Today this minister has so many people referred to him by the local doctor that he has been forced to limit the number of hours which he devotes to counseling, in order to give a balanced ministry to his church.

5. The pastor should devote special attention to the hospital in his community. Some ministerial associations have worked out a plan whereby the ministers in the community divide the responsibility for being on call for emergencies which arise in the local hospital. The plan reaches beyond church members to persons who have become inactive in their church affiliation, or who are not professing Christians but desire a minister in times of crisis. A good relationship with the personnel of the local hospital will also make the pastor's work with his own people more effective.

6. Any church of a thousand or more members should by all means have one staff member trained in religious counseling to give the major portion of his time to a personal ministry. The experience of hospital chaplains has proved that about thirty-five persons with emotional difficulties are all that one chaplain can deal with adequately along with his other duties. Certainly in a church with as many as a thousand members enough personal crises will arise among the membership to keep one man fully occupied with intensive counseling. It should be stated here that this work cannot be done adequately by an employed church visitor. Hospitals have already learned this fact. With all due respect for the fine work that is done by these women in welcoming strangers to the church, it is inescapably true that the minister's "role" is his most effective resource in his relationship with people who are in need of counseling.

7. The church can further enlarge its healing ministry by giving more attention to the principles of group psychotherapy which have been discovered in recent years. The book *So You Want to Help People* by Wittenberg should be required reading for every Sunday school teacher. Individuals of the same age level share many of the same emotional problems and adjustments, ranging from over-attachment to the mother at the nursery age to loneliness in the aged. The organizational machinery for group psychotherapy already exists in the church, but leadership must be trained if the psychological principles utilized in this form of therapy are to become tools for making Christianity more effective in the lives of people.

8. The church should make more use of the talent inherent in other professional people in the community. Dr. Hugh Brimm, who was for several years head of the Social Service Commission of the Southern Baptist Convention, has worked out an excellent program for Christian Home Week which utilizes various professional people. The family doctor, the lawyer, the social worker, the psychologist, the psychiatrist, the pediatrician, and members of related professions are assigned to lead certain age groups in a forty-five-minute discussion period concerned with practical problems of family life. The groups then meet together in the auditorium for a period of worship focused on family needs. The pastor of a Winston-Salem church directed a program of this type for his church and claims that it did more to revitalize his church than any special programs he had attempted thus far in his ministry.

Denominational bodies may foster an enlarged healing ministry in the following ways:

1. Some church groups, through their state missions program, are placing ministers in the larger cities to spend their full time working with patients of their own de-

nomination who come from adjoining counties to be treated in a medical center. If these men are well trained as counselors, pastors in the area could use their services to advantage by referring to them difficult problems which they encounter in their pastoral work.

2. Most progressive medical schools today have a department of preventive medicine. In the light of present-day knowledge of the human personality, the church can no longer neglect a preventive form of personal ministry. There seems little excuse for not having a full-time religious counselor on the campuses of church-related institutions such as colleges, seminaries, orphanages, hospitals, and nursing schools. Many a student has left such an institution, a failure, because no help was available to him in solving his personal difficulties. A student is never dropped from the School of Nursing at the North Carolina Baptist Hospital until she has had opportunity to confer with the chaplain, the psychiatrist, the psychologist, the medical doctor, or any other person who might be of help to her. Since this policy was instituted, the percentage of students who do not finish their training has greatly decreased. The case of Jane illustrates the effectiveness of this method in preventing humiliating failures.

Jane was having difficulty in getting along with her instructor as she did her ward work in the hospital. Whenever the instructor observed Jane as she worked, Jane would become so self-conscious and nervous that she could not do her work efficiently. This led to criticism on the part of the instructor, and eventually to a clash of personalities. After several hours of counseling, Jane revealed that her mother had yelled at her a thousand times or more, "Get on out of the house; I had rather do it myself than fool with you." When Jane was able to see that working closely with her supervisor, who was the authoritative figure in her life, had touched off the same emotional responses created in childhood by her mother's impatience, she was better able to cope with the problem. When the supervisor learned of this childhood background, she was more understanding of Jane's emotional difficulties.

3. Business executives should be led to see the value of employing chaplains in their industrial plants. An article in a recent issue of *The American Magazine* tells how the Reynolds Tobacco Company in Winston-Salem has benefited from the addition of a pastor-counselor to their organization.

In just two years religion-on-the-job has accomplished several pretty wonderful things. The morale of the company's 12,000 regular employees has improved to such an extent that old-timers say they actually "feel" the difference when they walk through factories and offices. Labor-management frictions which formerly existed in some departments have disappeared. Tensions between white and colored workers have diminished to the vanishing point. At the same time labor turnover has dropped from 7.61 to 5.22 per cent in two years, the accident rate has declined approximately 40 per cent, and absenteeism is much lower than it used to be. These three improvements cannot be attributed entirely to spiritual counseling, I was told, but company executives feel it has played a vital role in all of them. . . .

Chairman of the Board Gray is equally optimistic about the future possibilities of religion on the job. He thinks it would work just as well in many other industries as it has in the Reynolds Company. "I would not only recommend religious counseling for other companies," he told me; "I would crusade for it." [8]

4. Finally, church groups should foster legislation providing for the employment of chaplains in public institutions. The mental hospital, tuberculosis sanatorium, penal

---

[8] Clarence Woodbury, "They Put a Parson on the Payroll," *The American Magazine* (The Crowell-Collier Publishing Company) 1952, p. 81, 85.

institution, and school for delinquents ought to have a chaplain as a regular member of its staff. These institutions house people for whom Christ died.[9] Many of these people have been neglected and forgotten by the society from which they came and by their own families as well. Many states have already made considerable progress along this line. North Carolina, for example, is now in the process of placing chaplains in each of its state institutions.

With all the possibilities for an increased participation by the minister in the work of healing on the higher, more comprehensive levels of his denomination's organization, the healing ministry must largely rest upon the man in his immediate congregation and community. The pastor is most completely in his role when he is one who "knows" his people. Financial affairs of his members may be matter-of-course information in his possession. How many times the return of a patient to health is delayed by worry over medical and hospital bills!

Family relations, "in-law problems," the "problem child"—the pastor is no stranger to any of these. Many hospital patients are burdened with these satellite problems. The guilt, the unforgiving spirit, the anxiety can leave their marks on the course of the patient's recovery.

This is not to say that the general practitioner of medicine—"the family doctor"—does not frequently share such extensive and personal information about his patient. In times past, the family doctor has been considered in many localities as a one-man employment agency, financial advisor, father-confessor, marriage counselor, and friend-at-large. The increased demand for medical services as well as the emphasis upon specialization in recent years have served to limit the doctor's many-sided activities,

---

[9] Wayne E. Oates, *The Christian Pastor* (Philadelphia: The Westminster Press, 1950), p. 91.

however. He is usually the one man in the community who feels the pressure and the limitations of time when confronted with the extra-medical needs of his patients.

All of this is to say that the pastor can supplement and complement the doctor's work as they labor together in their local hospital. Because of his day-by-day contacts with his congregation, the pastor may have an even finer perspective of a patient's personality patterns, emotional drives, and will to live than the doctor has thus far acquired. In group meetings common to the life of his church the pastor is both interested participant and alert observer. Along with the interchange of opinions and ideas in the group he may note occasional angry exchanges or fleeting expressions of anxiety or depression. Subsequent "pastoral calls" may frequently have produced a wealth of material whose recalling in time of illness and sharing with the doctor may vitally affect the recovery and well-being of the patient. Incidents like the following occur frequently:

After a comparatively minor emergency operation in the local hospital a patient's behavior became quite a problem. Her complaints of unbearable pain were many. The sedation prescribed had virtually no effect.

At three o'clock on the morning after the operation her pastor was called to the hospital. The doctor explained briefly the problem and stated that he felt it unwise to prescribe more sedative. The pastor knew the patient to be a rather shy, uncommunicative person in her church groups. He was aware that the patient had had a morbid dread of hospitals from childhood, associated with the death of a sister in a hospital.

The pastor's presence in the sick room, because of previous relationships established with the patient in her home and in the church, brought an immediate calmness to the individual. As the patient quieted, the sedative took effect and the immediate problem was successfully met.

Subsequent interviews and visits by both doctor and minister while the patient was still in the hospital gave opportunity for facing realistically, and in the most appropriate setting, the deeper problem of anxiety.

Furthermore, the pastor can be a vital link in the patient's rehabilitation process as he returns to his home from the hospital. Through his contacts on a community-wide level, the pastor can often guide the patient to proper agencies and support his claims for help. Sometimes he must arrange through his church welfare-type aid for a family that proudly and fiercely refuses public assistance. Here especially his insights into the patient's personality and his family situation and background are invaluable.

Where a long period of invalidism or a permanent physical handicap are indicated the pastor is particularly challenged to supply an intelligent, insightful ministry that will produce the best results for the patient. The dictum may be stated positively and dogmatically that in these situations the pastor should not make use of sentimental pious platitudes. The pastor is wise indeed who recognizes the possibility of doing serious emotional damage, regardless of his high motives, when his approach to the crisis situations in illness is not undergirded by factual knowledge of the situation at hand. At best, the skilled pastor can work with the doctors and contribute to the total welfare of the patient. At worst, he can get in the doctor's way, hinder the patient's recovery and possibly do serious damage to the patient's emotional balance. In view of this fact it is well for the pastor to think seriously about his relationship to other members of the professional team.

Chapter Two

THE PASTOR AND HOSPITAL
PERSONNEL

Today, a large portion of the pastor's ministry to the sick is performed in the hospital in his community. The general hospital is a highly professionalized environment. The administrator, the business manager, the pharmacist, the laboratory technician, the dietitian, the nurse, the doctor, and others are constantly working together for the general welfare of the patient. The effectiveness of the pastor's ministry depends largely upon his ability to co-ordinate his services with the work of other professional people in the hospital where he is visiting. The nurse, the physician, and the psychiatrist are the members of the healing team with whom the minister will be most closely associated.

The Pastor and the Nurse

Relationship between the pastor and the nurse is extremely important, because the nurse has made a vital place for herself as a member of the healing team. It would be impossible for a minister to work effectively in a local hospital without the fullest co-operation from the nursing staff; and the medical profession, likewise, leans heavily upon its sister profession. Over and over again the hospital chaplain hears a doctor make the statement, "The favorable prognosis is largely due to the good nursing care the patient has received." Since the nurse is in and out of the patient's room many times during the course of a day, she can be of tremendous help to the minister.

Her close supervision of the patient makes it possible for the nurse to observe the sick person's various emotional reactions. Such attitudes as are expressed in concern for husband or children, homesickness, and fear of hospital procedures are rarely recorded on the patient's charts. Yet these mild emotional responses can be the cue that leads to a vital Christian ministry by the pastor. Some of his best "timed" visits are made at the suggestion of an observant nurse, who may mention to him that "Mr. Jones seems to be a little unhappy. I believe a visit from you might help." Therefore, the pastor should get to know as many of the nurses in the local hospital as possible. When his time in the hospital is limited, he can often find which of his parishioners are most in need of a pastoral visit by stopping at the desk and asking the nurse in charge how the various patients from his congregation are getting along. Two or three visits made to people who need him can accomplish far more than eight or ten "pop calls" made at random.

The ideal way for the minister to become acquainted with the nurses in the local hospital is to use any opportunity which arises to come before them as a group. Where there is a nursing school connected with the hospital, the minister may let the director of the school know that he will be glad to lead vesper services for the students from time to time. One pastor in North Carolina has made a place in his church program for the students from the school of nursing in his community and is teaching a two-hour course in psychology of nursing which is scheduled in the school curriculum. Not only does this minister have a pastoral relationship with these students, but through them he has a more effective relationship with patients in the hospital. These nurses are in close contact with every patient in the hospital, and their sensitivity to the patient's needs makes them of inestimable value to the pastor in his hospital ministry.

The pastor should remember, in his contacts with the nursing staff, that it is the nurse's responsibility to protect and manage the patient. Therefore, if for no reason other than that of courtesy, the minister should ask the nurse's permission before going behind any closed door in the hospital.

It is a good practice for the pastor to go to the nurse's desk and ask her about certain existing conditions before working within her area of responsibility. For example, the nurse can tell him where the doctors have finished making rounds; or if it is early in the morning, she can point out the rooms in which the patients have received their morning baths and are prepared for a visit. Then, too, the nurse can often avoid disturbing the pastor when she knows where he is visiting.

As a general rule, the minister should excuse himself when the nurse comes around with medication. The patient may wish to speak to the nurse about an intimate matter, or the nursing procedure might be of such a personal nature that the nurse would have to ask any visitor to leave the room. Usually, if the nurse wishes the pastor to remain, she will indicate that fact.

The pastor should make use of every opportunity to aid the nurse in her work. Many difficult situations arising in a general hospital must be handled with great diplomacy and patience. Some families are inconsiderate about observing visiting hours; often it is difficult to persuade relatives to leave the room at the time of a death; or an "ornery" patient who is demanding too much attention and is criticizing the nurse for not giving it may need a visit from the minister. The nurse will be grateful to the pastor when he can help care for situations of this kind.

It should be emphasized that, in order to keep a good working relationship with the nursing staff, as well as with the doctors, the pastor should let them know where he may be called and should make every effort to follow up the requests for pastoral visits which he receives. If he cannot answer a call to see a patient, he should explain to the person who made the request why it cannot be carried out. Otherwise, if a doctor or nurse tries to get a pastor several times and fails, he or she will gradually stop making the effort to call him.

The Pastor and the Doctor

Equally as important as his relationship with the nursing staff is the pastor's relationship with the medical doctor in the environment of a general hospital. The value that lies in co-operation between the minister and the doctor has long been recognized and has been mentioned in practically all the books that have been written on the pastoral office. Washington Gladden said: "In the first place the pastor should be careful to co-operate in every possible way with the attending physician, to whom belongs the chief responsibility, and whose orders should be scrupulously respected." [10] A pertinent statement made by Charles Reynolds Brown in 1900 also reveals considerable insight into this subject. "The most friendly relations and the highest form of co-operation between the doctor of medicine and the minister of religion can best be secured where both realize that each one has an entirely distinct function to perform for the service of humanity and where both realize that each can best aid the other by attending strictly to his own specialty." [11]

[10] Washington Gladden, *The Christian Pastor* (New York: Charles Scribner's Sons, 1898), p. 187.

[11] Charles F. Kemp, *Physicians of the Soul* (New York: The Macmillan Company, 1947), p. 236.

It is the systematic and recorded study made jointly by the two professions that is of recent origin. The book which has become a classic in this connection—*The Art of Ministering to the Sick* by Richard C. Cabot and Russell L. Dicks—was first published in 1936 and still offers valuable help for the pastor today. It pointed the way toward co-operation in the healing ministry.

The common meeting ground between the minister and the doctor is in the area of the patient's emotions. A satisfactory relationship rests upon a recognition by both the doctor and the minister that each one has a distinct function to perform. Each has a unique role founded in tradition and placed upon him automatically by the expectancy of the patient. It is in one's own role that one functions best. For example, it is an indisputable fact that a confession to a minister has a cathartic effect which does not necessarily result if the confession is made to a doctor; and if the blood pressure or temperature falls and the nerves are steadied, the patient has been helped. Likewise, the doctor who tells a patient that there is nothing wrong with his heart can alleviate anxiety which the minister could never touch. Therefore, as these illustrations indicate, there must necessarily be some overlapping in the work of the two professions.

Untold damage has been done to the physician-clergy relationship by the ignorance and prejudice of extremists in both professions. There are individual ministers and doctors who seem to feel that they have the final answer and are prejudiced from the beginning against any co-operation. The following incidents represent extreme examples in both professions.

A minister came into the North Carolina Baptist Hospital and visited in a four-bed ward without speaking to a nurse or doctor and, therefore, had no knowledge of the condition of the patients in the ward. Three of the patients were waiting for thyroid operations, and one in particular had for five days been under special treatment designed to quiet her nerves sufficiently to prepare her for operation. The hyperthyroid patient is easily excited because of his organic condition, and in ten minutes after the minister entered the room he had what he thought was an old-fashioned revival meeting in progress. During his prayer two of the patients started clapping their hands and shouting at the top of their voices. The nurse and doctor soon arrived on the scene. The minister resented their interference, and they resented his even more. In this case the minister had resources which could aid the doctor, but because of his lack of knowledge he did more harm than good. One sometimes wonders which is the more ineffective: zeal without knowledge or knowledge without zeal.

An example at the opposite extreme is the case of a young man twenty-two years of age who sought a minister's help on an emotional problem. When asked if he had been to a physician, he said, "Yes, but I was even more upset by the advice I was given. The doctor said if I would go out and have promiscuous sex relations, it would help me to grow up. But my conscience rebels against such a thing. I have been a regular attendant at church all my life, and I know that the doctor is wrong." Of course the majority of doctors as well as ministers know that, whereas this boy had one "devil" to begin with, he would have had seven if he had followed this doctor's advice.

Hospital chaplains working in close harmony with doctors day in and day out are in a key position to help create a better understanding between the two professions. The chaplain's position is even more strategic when he is in a teaching institution where many doctors are serving internships before going into practice. A still greater opportunity exists when the hospital chaplain is responsible from time to time for the training of theological students in the same environment.

What are some "rules of conduct" by which the pastor should be governed in his relationship to the doctor?

First, he should, as has already been pointed out, work in close harmony with the physician. If the minister discovers something in the emotional life of a patient that seems to have a direct bearing upon his illness, he should, for the sake of the patient's welfare, make this information known to the doctor. In most instances pertinent facts can be given the physician without violating the patient's confidence. If necessary, the patient can be encouraged to tell the story to the doctor, or can be asked, "Do you mind if I talk this over with your doctor?" A patient may tell things to the doctor that he would not think of revealing to the minister, and *vice versa.* Furthermore, the pastor in his visiting may, more or less incidentally, learn some important bit of information that the doctor has not had time to discover.

The pastor should never have more than one or two lengthy talks with a hospitalized patient concerning some problem in his life without discussing the matter with the patient's doctor. Frequently an individual, under the stress of an illness, will desire to discuss emotional problems with his pastor and will become upset during the process. In his relationship with the patient the pastor should keep in mind always that the patient entered the hospital to see the doctor and not to see him.

Second, a precaution for the pastor to observe in his relationship with the physician has been expressed by Washington Gladden as follows: "The pastor should be very careful about volunteering medical advice; the cases are rare in which he should venture any suggestion which would have the effect to weaken the confidence of the patient or his friends in the physician in charge." [12] If this was good advice for the pastor in Gladden's day, it is even more pertinent for the pastor visiting in a hospital today. There is absolutely no occasion for the pastor to prescribe some home remedy in a hospital environment. There will be many occasions, however, when the pastor will be able to strengthen the confidence of the patient in his doctor, a factor which is often essential to the success of treatment. In many instances the patient in a medical center does not know all the doctors working on his case. Therefore, the pastor should seek every opportunity to make the patient feel that he is in competent hands and is receiving the best available care. Such assurance can help him respond positively to treatment.

The complaint most often heard from the patient in a hospital connected with a teaching institution is that of not seeing the "head doctor." The pastor can in sincerity assure the patient of the doctor's over-all supervision of his case. In this connection the minister should not enter into detailed discussion concerning the distinction between the senior medical student, the intern, and the doctor in charge. In the majority of instances the patient is not aware of any distinction. In fact, on one occasion the chief of staff in a teaching hospital was obliged to call a senior medical student, who had had previous contact with the patient, to come in and advise an operation before the patient would consent to it.

As far as possible the minister should refrain from any discussion of the nature of the patient's illness. This is strictly the area of the physician, and there are no occasions for the pastor to discuss with the patient what he can expect in the course of his illness. If the question of the patient's illness arises, as it frequently does, the pastor's

[12] Washington Gladden, *The Christian Pastor and the Working Church* (New York: Charles Scribner's and Sons, 1898), p. 187.

safest plan is to ask, "What has your doctor told you about this?" or "Have you talked this over with your doctor?"

Third, another precaution which the minister should observe in his relationship with the doctor is the avoidance of medical terms. The pastor who visits daily in a hospital becomes superficially familiar with many such terms. The doctor dislikes his employment of these terms, however, just as much as the minister resents encroachment into his own field with a basic lack of knowledge. As Cabot says:

Ministers win doctors' approval by deeds, not by words. An action that shows devotion, courage, foresight, imagination, tact, self-sacrifice, will win the doctor's admiration as soon as any one else's. The minister who listens well and learns well wins the confidence of the physician.[13]

Fourth, when the doctor approaches on his morning rounds while the pastor is visiting with a patient, the latter should courteously excuse himself and leave the room. The patient in the hospital is anxious to see his doctor and usually looks forward with a great deal of anticipation to his visit. As everyone should know, the intimacy of this contact does not warrant the pastor's presence.

Fifth, the minister should remember that he can aid the doctor greatly by working with the families of patients in many situations. Especially will his services to the family be appreciated when a death occurs. The pastor's ministry here will win the appreciation of the doctor for the pastor's ministry.

Finally, the pastor must come to some decision regarding autopsies. Not only for the sake of co-operation with the medical profession but because of the values that accrue to medical science from postmortem studies, the

---

[13] Richard C. Cabot and Russell L. Dicks, *The Art of Ministering to the Sick* (New York: The Macmillan Company, 1936) p. 50.

pastor should add his influence to that of the doctor in persuading the family to consent to an autopsy when it is requested. The family expects the doctor to request an autopsy, but a word from the minister as to its teaching value sometimes causes them to give assent when previously they had refused. The pastor can be especially helpful in removing any religiously grounded fears which the family may have concerning this procedure. Naturally he should not bring undue pressure to bear which would cause a family to consent against their will.

Dr. Wingate Johnson, of North Carolina, has given the medical viewpoint on the minister's relation to the physician in the following hints for good doctor-minister relations.

"1. Don't be offended if denied admission to the patient's room at some particular time. He may have had a sedative preliminary to an operation; or he may be too uncomfortable from nausea or pain to talk; or there may be some other reason why he should not be disturbed.

"2. Don't stay too long. A sick person becomes tired easily.

"3. Be cheerful but not boisterous. Remember 2 Timothy 1:7: 'For God hath not given us the spirit of fear; but of power, and of love, and of a sound mind.'

"4. Don't let your visit be a pathological conference. If the patient's illness reminds you of other similar cases, be sure that they had happy endings before you mention them to him.

"5. Don't attempt to prescribe for the patient's physical symptoms. The pastor's interest should be primarily in the patient's spiritual problems, which are in his domain, while the physical symptoms are the doctor's responsibility.

"6. Don't suggest a change of doctors. Never say anything to lessen the patient's confidence in his doctor, which is a big factor in his recovery. You may be greatly tempted, through loyalty to your own doctor or to one who is a faithful member of your church, to hint that he is particularly skilful in treating the condition from which the patient suffers, but to yield to this temptation is to invite trouble.

"7. One of the most common mistakes made by pastors —from the doctor's viewpoint—is to fall a prey to irregular practitioners. Even if you believe in one yourself, don't attempt to foist your belief on others. Remember that medical cults bear exactly the same relation to the regular practice of medicine that 'holy rollers' do to the more widely accepted churches. Unfortunately irregular practitioners are very apt to pose as great church workers."

The pastor can learn a great deal from the Christian doctor that will be of value to him in his ministry to the sick. Andrew W. Blackwood, after spending six weeks as a patient in a hospital, wrote in his book on *Pastoral Work:*

The local pastor should be as skillful as a physician. If the writer were a man of wealth he would establish a fund for the clinical training of prospective pastors. The course would be given at a general hospital. There the student of pastoral theology would work for six or eight weeks under a Christian physician, as well as a mature nurse. Starting out as an orderly, and then serving as a sort of semi-medical intern, he would look at the patient through the eyes of a man with a "healing presence." This line of thought was suggested to the author by a recent experience of six weeks abed in the Presbyterian Hospital at Philadelphia, under the care of a physician like the One of Galilee.[14]

The following paragraph from Carroll Wise is an appropriate conclusion for this discussion of the pastor's relation to the physician.

---

[14] Andrew W. Blackwood, *Pastoral Work—A Source Book for Ministers* (Philadelphia: The Westminster Press, 1945), p. 24.

Not since the rise of scientific medicine has a point been developed which offers such a sound basis for physician-clergyman relationships. The organism-environment concept in medicine both broadens and deepens the concept of illness and health so that the place and function of various professional workers become clarified and the interrelationship of these workers is seen in a more helpful perspective.[15]

The Pastor and the Psychiatrist

The psychoanalyst and psychiatrist have been largely responsible for the new emphasis upon the mind-body relationship in medical science. Not all hospitals have psychiatrists on their medical staffs as yet, but it is probably only a matter of time until most large hospitals will have at least one representative of this specialty on their staffs. Hence, it is in order to discuss here the role of the pastor in relation to the psychiatrist in the hospital setting. The psychiatrist, of course, is a medical doctor who specializes in mental and emotional problems. All that has been said concerning the pastor's relation to the medical doctor is equally applicable to his relationship with the psychiatrist. The minister and the psychiatrist are working more nearly in the same general area, however, since both are dealing with the individual's basic approach to life. For this reason the necessity for co-operation between them is intensified.

An understanding of the relationship which should exist between the pastor and the psychiatrist in the general hospital requires a comparison of the aims and methods of the two professions and of the basic assumptions which underlie their methods and aims. Such a comparison, however, serves only as a background for the question with which we are chiefly concerned: Just how can the pastor and the psychiatrist co-operate with each other in a general hospital? Thus far, discussions on psychiatric and

---

[15] Carroll Wise, *Religion in Illness and Health* (New York: Harper and Brothers Publishers, 1942), p. 265.

pastoral collaborations have been confined chiefly to articles in professional journals, and the main emphasis in these articles has been upon differences and similarities in the two professions. Nevertheless, it is gratifying to note that institutes on religion and psychiatry are being held in various parts of the country.

Several outstanding figures in the fields of religion and medicine have contributed to the understanding of this subject. Seward Hiltner, associate professor of pastoral theology at the University of Chicago, presented at the Temple-Israel Institute on Religion and Psychiatry held in Boston in October, 1947, a paper entitled "Five Areas of Mutual Endeavor." [16] In it he discussed five points at which psychiatry and religion meet today: the clinic, the centers of education, the community, the patient or parishioner, and the church. By "clinic" he referred to any hospital, prison, out-patient service, or agency where the psychiatrist has the responsibility for the total welfare of the patient. Hiltner pointed out that more chaplains in such clinical settings and ministers in training for the chaplaincy are to be found today than at any previous time, and that physicians are showing less therapeutic imperialism and more willingness to recognize the capacity of other workers, such as the minister, to give psychotherapeutic help to people. Thus, the minister and psychiatrist each has his own clearly defined focus of function, but there is a rather broad overlapping and borderline territory.

Otis Rice, religious director of St. Luke's Hospital in New York, has pointed out several areas of sound agreement between the two disciplines. Both agree upon the sacredness of the integrity of the individual personality and the terrible danger of violating this integrity. Both Christianity and psychotherapy are optimistic regarding

---

[16] Joshua Loth Liebman, editor, *Psychiatry and Religion* (Boston: The Beacon Press, 1948), pp. 3–17.

the potentialities inherent in many human situations and would probably agree that the forces and resources within the life situation are to be trusted. Then, too, there seems to be growing agreement that behavior has meaning if one but has the data to understand it—in other words, the dynamic view of personality and the concept of unconscious motivation offer new tools and responsibilities.[17]

David Roberts, professor of philosophy of religion at the Union Theological Seminary, says that co-operation between religion and psychotherapy is still hampered by the hostility with which religious thinkers greeted Freud, and also by the effects of what he had to say about religion, but that there are those within both psychiatric and Christian groups who have found harmonization between religious faith and mental health to be not only possible but almost inescapable. For collaboration, both fields must lay aside rigid preconceptions and move out of an atmosphere of argumentative debate into an atmosphere of mutual search. He urges churchmen to stop criticizing psychoanalysis upon the basis of secondhand information and their knowledge of bunglers and charlatans in the field. On the other hand, he argues that if the psychiatrist will become active in church affairs, he will find the church and its beliefs to differ widely from the versions of religion encountered in the mentally ill patient.[18]

Some of the well-known psychiatrists in America today have also expressed themselves on the subject of religion and its relation to psychiatry. Karl A. Menninger, in reply to criticisms leveled at the first edition of his book, *The Human Mind,* has said:

Psychiatrists would be egotistical indeed to believe that they have any "corner" on the art or science of counselling the un-

---

[17] Otis Rice, "Christianity and Psychotherapy: Conflict or Cooperation," *Journal of Pastoral Care,* 3:12–16 Fall-Winter, 1949.

[18] David E. Roberts, "Cooperation Between Religion and Psychotherapy," *Pastoral Psychology,* 1:23–27. No. 4, May, 1950.

happy or correcting the misguided. Unless they set themselves up to be the very high priests of civilization, which, of course, they do not, they cannot assume to be the final authority in telling people how to live.[19]

In answer to the question, "What would you do if you were a minister?" he offers some very practical suggestions:

First of all I should acquaint myself with what is known scientifically about the human personality. . . . I should familiarize myself with the particular ways in which religion or something which passes for religion is grasped at in an irrational, compulsive way by certain individuals whose maladjustment is not apparent. . . . If I were a minister I would study with the psychiatrist some of those instances in which religion has seemed to do harm rather than good for the individual; I should study them without prejudice and without fear. . . . Finally, or perhaps first of all, I should inquire of myself, were I a minister, just what my motives, my deepest purposes, were in the pursuit of my calling.[20]

As to the future, Menninger says:

It is too early to say what the future developments of the practical application of psychiatry to the work of the clergyman will be, nor can I attempt in these pages to review the more theoretical side of the connections between religion and psychiatry. There are many people in the world to be helped, and even the most agnostic scientist should concede that what is genuinely helpful to people cannot be denied them. Psychiatry and religion may be thought of as cooperative rather than antagonistic.[21]

William B. Terhune, the psychiatrist, has stressed the fact that man is made up of three inseparable components —body, mind, and spirit—and that when any one of these

---

[19] Karl A. Menninger, *The Human Mind* (New York: Alfred A. Knopf, 1948, third edition), p. 460.
[20] *Ibid.*, pp. 463–469.
[21] *Ibid.*, pp. 473–474.

three function inadequately the result is illness. Religion and psychiatry do not conflict as they strive for the same purpose—the oneness of man with the universe. The misunderstandings between physicians and priests are due to misinterpretation of the purpose and processes of religion as well as psychiatry. According to Terhune, the unsubstantiated suggestion of conflict between psychiatry and religion is due to two factors:

One: At times science is wrong in its theories, but these errors are of short duration and are soon corrected. Two: In some instances the Church has incorporated erroneous scientific conclusions in religion, and refuses to correct these errors.[22]

Terhune declared that greater co-operation between the two disciplines is necessary and stated that some of the failures of psychiatry are due to its failure to recognize that the spirit of man is as essential to his health as are his body and mind.[23]

Leon Yochelson, a practicing psychoanalyst associated with the Washington School of Psychiatry, considers psychiatry and religion as having one common denominator:

Psychiatry, briefly, is the study of man in the frame of reference of interpersonal relationships. Religion has to do with man's attitude towards God, man and the universe. In examining these two statements we find one common denominator, man's relation to man. It is here that our professions operate at the same level. It is here surely, that we can work as colleagues, in a joint effort to study man amongst men,—to study and strive for the dignity of man.[24]

---

[22] William B. Terhune, M.D., "Religion and Psychiatry," *The Journal of Pastoral Care*, 2:3, Fall, 1948, p. 15.

[23] *Ibid.*, pp. 19, 20.

[24] Leon Yochelson, M.D., "Psychiatric and Pastoral Collaboration with Reference to Schizophrenia," *Journal of Clinical Pastoral Work*, 1:31, Spring, 1949, p. 25.

Yochelson thinks that the cleft between the two professions in the past has been due to the hostility toward religion discerned in the writings of Freud, to misunderstanding arising out of the emphasis upon sexuality in psychiatric literature, and to the controversy concerning guilt and sin. Nevertheless, he believes that the two groups not only *can* work together, but *must*. The necessity for co-operation is illustrated in the case of a catatonic schizophrenic—a person confronting overwhelming anxiety and expending tremendous effort to find a means of overcoming this anxiety. The condition seems to result from the double jeopardy of guilt and extreme loneliness, which join forces to crush what is probably an already vulnerable self-esteem. Yochelson believes that the psychiatrist and minister can join hands here to interfere in the patient's morbid process. "Where we clearly join hands, I think, is in much of the current anxiety experienced by reason of the loneliness itself." [25]

These statements by men of recognized authority in both religion and psychiatry make it clear that, thus far, only limited progress has been made toward co-operation between the two professions. Therefore, for the sake of future progress, the minister and the psychiatrist must both avoid the temptation of acting in a "prima donna" role or of attempting to "play God" to persons seeking their help. Probably no other individuals in society wield as much influence or speak with such authority as do the minister and doctor. One is believed capable of pointing the way to eternal life, while the other offers men their best hope of prolonging their days on earth. The minister who enjoys an "authoritarian role" is likely to look upon psychiatry as a threat or an intrusion into his field, while the psychiatrist who believes that religious experience is an unconscious wish-fulfilment and that God is only a projection of the

---

[25] *Ibid.*, p. 28.

father-image, plays God for his patient and sees religion as a conflicting element.[26]

Nevertheless, the interest manifested in the pastoral care movement in this country today is evidence that many ministers are seeking scientific tools to make their ministry more effective. Moreover, many psychiatrists are showing a willingness to co-operate by accepting invitations to write articles for religious journals or to appear on programs planned to foster better understanding between the two professions.

Every member of the department of psychiatry at the Bowman Gray School of Medicine and the North Carolina Baptist Hospital has expressed a keen interest in the clinical training program for ministers sponsored by these institutions. Psychiatrists have readily volunteered their services in leading seminars and lecturing to the groups and have been most co-operative in relation to work with patients in the hospital. Dr. Angus Randolph invites theological interns into his psychiatric clinic, where a psychiatrist, a psychiatric social worker, a psychologist, a medical doctor, a nurse, and a chaplain work as a team. As head of the team, Dr. Randolph makes the necessary diagnostic studies and then schedules certain patients for interviews with the minister in training, who has access to help from all the other members of the team. On the basis of the results obtained with this plan, Dr. Randolph feels that the chaplain, because of his role as a minister, is often less frightening to the patient, can establish a relationship with him, and can help interpret to him the aid that the other members of the team have to offer. Even more important in this comprehensive approach to the patient's problem is the fact that the minister's training fits him for helping the patient to acquire a philosophy of life which will en-

[26] Wayne E. Oates, *The Christian Pastor* (Philadelphia: The Westminster Press, 1950), pp. 26–42.

able him to continue his growth toward a plane of grace, where he can love his neighbor as himself.

Articles upon the subject of co-operation between the minister and the psychiatrist have their place, but face-to-face contact in a joint effort to solve a difficult life situation will provide the final answer to mutual understanding between the two professions.

The hospital chaplain in the clinical setting is in a strategic position to make a contribution toward greater co-operation between the two fields of endeavor in the future. In the clinical setting representatives of religion and members of the psychiatric professions are in a face-to-face relationship, using the same set of clinical facts in many instances, and observing each other's methods and goals. As a result of this opportunity for observation and personal acquaintance, many of the barriers mentioned in the foregoing discussions fall away and greater understanding results. As Robert Preston has said:

A small slice of psychotherapy taken out of context can be made to look ridiculous. The same is true of isolated religious precepts. When working along with a psychiatrist, a chaplain will see the total perspective and goal of therapy.[27]

The hospital chaplain can do much to bridge the gap between the psychiatrist in the clinic and the minister out in the community. He is in a position to enlist the psychiatrist's aid in cases where the minister is having difficulty in recognizing the nature of a parishioner's problem and does not know where to turn for help. Such cases not only serve to educate the minister regarding psychiatry, but also enhance his appreciation of an ally in many of the predicaments in which he finds himself.

The pastor is in a strategic position in the community to

---

[27] Robert A. Preston, "A Chaplain Looks at Psychiatry," *The Journal of Clinical Pastoral Work*, 2:172, number 4, Winter, 1949.

forward co-operation between the two professions. Since he deals with "value judgments," the minister is an influential person in the community in shaping human behavior and attitudes. He cannot ignore the psychiatrist if the discoveries in mental hygiene are integrated into the community life for the good of humanity.

Further discussion of interprofessional co-operation in this chapter is based upon the assumption that the pastor has a clear conception of his focus of function and a basic appreciation of his role as a minister. If the psychiatrist likewise recognizes his focus of function, then both can move out of the realm of philosophical debate concerning the two fields of thought and meet together in the mental processes of the maladjusted patient to augment each other's services for his good.

The following suggestions may help the pastor to co-operate with the psychiatrist in the local hospital and community. It should be emphasized first of all, however, that the minister, to be most effective, needs some training in pastoral care. This can best be obtained in a clinical setting where guidance is available from an experienced hospital chaplain.

1. The pastor should get to know the psychiatrist in his community as a person. Because psychiatry and religion have not yet learned to co-operate as they should, the pastor's approach as he visits in the local hospital setting will depend almost entirely upon his ability to penetrate professional façades and establish friendly relations with the psychiatrist.

2. The psychiatrist will determine the diagnosis. It should be noted, however, that in occasional cases when the patient's religious ideas or beliefs are on the border line between the so-called normal and abnormal, the training of the pastor in the history of religious sects can be helpful in making the distinction. Anton T. Boisen has

pointed out the close relationship between some forms of mental disorder and certain types of religious experience.

I think that I have shown that certain types of mental disorder are closely related to certain types of religious experience and that a consideration of the one throws light upon the other. I have also sought to show that in the experiences of the mentally ill there are operative those profound and delicate laws of the spiritual life with which theology deals.[28]

A study on psychoses among followers of Father Divine by Bender and Yarrell at the Bellevue Psychopathic Hospital in New York City reveals the same close relationship:

We have reported here 18 cases of individuals who have come under our observation and who have been associated with the Father Divine Movement. Two of these were women who were accused of neglecting their children because of the teachings of Father Divine that family life should not be recognized. One of the women had even refused a widow's pension claiming that God would provide. Nevertheless, it was felt that neither of these women were psychotic because their beliefs were not different from those of the teachings of Father Divine and they showed no unusual emotional reactions or other psychotic symptoms. Eight of the cases we have classified as manic depressive psychosis. This group of cases are of special interest since it has been possible to trace the mechanisms of the psychosis through the religious experiences.[29]

The so-called normal participants at his meeting are not far removed from the psychotic cases which are brought to the hospital, or perhaps we may say, that some of the so-called psychotic individuals are not far removed from the normal worshippers.[30]

---

[28] Anton T. Boisen, *The Exploration of the Inner World, A Study of Mental Disorder and Religious Experience,* (New York: Willett, Clark and Company, 1936), pp. 22.

[29] Lauretta Bender and Zulika Yarrell, "Psychosis Among Followers of Father Divine," *Journal of Nervous and Mental Disorder,* 87:443, No. 4, April, 1938.

[30] *Ibid.,* p. 432.

3. The psychiatrist will also determine the deeper dynamics involved in the patient's illness which will govern the therapeutic approach, and the pastor will be guided by the psychiatrist's findings as he attempts to use his religious role in dealing with the mental processes of the patient. It is probably at this point that the co-operative venture is likely to meet the greatest strain. Edith Weigert points out that "from the viewpoint of psychiatry, sin is a psychogenic illness." [31] Thus the problem of different terminologies— the barrier of semantics—must be overcome before real co-operation and understanding can exist between the pastor and the psychiatrist. Weigert further states, however, that there are common denominators which can become the basis of sound agreement. She mentions three common denominators of sinfulness and psychogenic illness: (1) isolation, (2) their compulsive character, (3) the fact that both produce guilt feelings and shame. "Last year, when I participated in a case seminar with ministers, I found that a psychiatrist and a theologian can arrive at mutual understanding and overcome the barrier of semantics." [32]

It is in the realm of these "common denominators" that the greatest benefits can be derived from interprofessional co-operation, provided understanding exists. As the pastor and the psychiatrist, each in his distinctive role, move side by side into the mental processes of the patient, values accrue from this relationship that do not exist in the single-handed approach. Not only is the pastor's work made more effective by his access to the psychiatrist's interpretation of the deeper dynamics involved, but each can serve to enhance and support the role of the other.

4. The pastor may help to increase the individual's faith in the psychiatrist. Most laymen still have little conception

---

[31] Edith H. Weigert, M.D., "Psychiatry and Sin," *The Journal of Pastoral Care*, 4:43, Numbers 1 and 2, Spring-Summer, 1950.
[32] *Ibid.*, p. 45.

of the vast importance of the mind-body relationship. Often resistance is met when the patient in a general hospital is told that a psychiatrist is to see him for consultation and treatment. When such an attitude is found, or when hostility arises after a psychiatric consultation, the pastor, as one outside the medical profession, is able to give support to the doctors and encourage the patient to accept the psychiatric interpretation.

5. In some instances the process of healing can be speeded up when the patient has access to both minister and psychiatrist at the same time. Especially is this true when the patient is unable to incorporate into his religious belief some explanation of human nature. Likewise the patient who is fighting loneliness and guilt and who feels "cut off from the land of the living" will have an easier road back to a feeling of oneness with his fellows if he finds acceptance in a structural relationship involving a minister and a doctor.

6. Teamwork between the pastor and the psychiatrist can be especially vital when the patient feels that his condition is a reflection upon his Christian faith. In many instances ministers or religious workers, because of their religious beliefs, feel a sense of guilt at the thought of taking a personal problem to someone outside the realm of their religion. They feel this to be a reflection upon their Christian life. That this idea is erroneous does not invalidate the point under discussion. By way of illustration, this writer has counseled with another minister, encouraged psychiatric help for him, and then formed a team with the psychiatrist in which the chaplain and psychiatrist sat together with the minister for eight-hour-long interviews. During these joint discussions the psychiatrist handled the mental mechanisms of personality adjustment, and the chaplain gave support to the minister in what he was doing and aided in the interpretation of factors involving the

minister's relationship to his denomination and his theological beliefs.

7. The patient whose illness seems to be directly connected with certain religious manifestations can often be guided to a more healthy rehabilitation by having access to a minister who works alongside the psychiatrist. When a patient comes into the general hospital in a feverish state of mind, preoccupied with the Bible, religious tracts, and the winning of fellow patients to Christ, the practice among most psychiatrists is to take all religious literature from him immediately. This is done because the patient in his present state of mind is not capable of being objective, but tends to identify himself with whatever religious ideas are encountered. In some patients preoccupation with religion is motivated by a deep religious concern, while in others it may be just another escape mechanism. Regardless of the reason for this preoccupation, however, the person must find a substitute response. The minister can be a substitute for the religious literature, a person to whom the patient can react during his treatment. There may be, of course, stages in the illness during which the presence of the minister's role will serve only to agitate the patient; but unless the patient has an opportunity to work through these religious feelings at some time in his rehabilitation, the process has not been complete. The patient returns to his environment and to the religious fervor of his group no more able than before to cope with the problem that helped to create the form of expression his illness followed in the beginning.

8. When the pastor recommends psychiatric help to an individual with whom he has a relationship, a brief referral note should be written to the psychiatrist about that person. There may be some facts about the individual's family situation or community life which, when presented objectively by someone other than the person involved, may be

of help to the psychiatrist in his diagnosis and treatment of his case. Such a referral note should touch on the following points: (1) the onset of the illness, (2) the individual's family constellation, (3) his school adjustment, (4) his social adjustment, (5) his marital adjustment, (6) his religious adjustment, (7) the community's reaction toward the person. The note will be of much greater value if it gives only essential facts and does not contain irrelevant details or theories of the writer.

9. Co-operation between the minister and the psychiatrist can be especially valuable when the patient is released from the hospital and returns to his community. A brief note from the psychiatrist to the patient's pastor concerning the individual's abilities and needs with regard to his adjustment process would be helpful. Most communities still need to be educated to a better understanding of mental and emotional illness. It is unfortunate that a stigma is often attached to the person receiving psychiatric treatment; he is so much in need of understanding and acceptance. The pastor, by setting an example of friendly helpfulness toward the recently discharged psychiatric patient and by helping the individual become acclimated to the community again, can do much to aid in establishing a permanent cure. The patient may need to find new avenues of expression for energies once turned in upon himself. Church work offers many wholesome outlets for such energies.

10. Finally, the minister and the psychiatrist must not fail to co-operate in making available to the public the rules of preventive mental hygiene. Psychiatrists have busy schedules, but most of them would be willing to help if they were asked by a minister to come to his church and lead a forum for young people.

Dr. Lloyd Thompson, head of the department of psychiatry at the Bowman Gray School of Medicine, originated the idea in the Winston-Salem area of holding weekly classes for expectant mothers. A psychiatrist, psychologist, social worker, pediatrician, community health nurse, and minister lecture to these classes, which have all been well attended. These classes meet in churches in the downtown area of Winston-Salem, rotating each week from one church to another.

Team co-operation between the pastor and the psychiatrist is the ideal to work toward, but much work must be done before it will be widely accepted by psychiatrists and ministers as a worthy goal. Any minister visiting in a hospital, no matter how well he is trained for the task, should recognize this fact. His philosophy may be perfect, but failure will be inevitable if he is unrelaxed, too assertive, and overanxious to prove his theories and their worth. The existence of such an attitude, of course, is fundamentally dependent upon his concept of himself. The pastor should not expect every member of the medical profession to be sold on the team idea and should remember that to take a defensive attitude will defeat his whole purpose. If the pastor cannot gradually and unobtrusively demonstrate his effectiveness, then he has no right to be on the healing team.

Chapter Three

VISITING THE SICK

Every person employed by a general hospital has a specific job to do, and each job is distinctively related to the over-all purpose of the institution. That purpose is to promote the welfare of the patient, or in other words, to get him well as quickly as possible. In order that this purpose may be accomplished, it is necessary for every person in the hospital to do his work in such a manner as to create the least amount of friction with other jobs and persons involved. Therefore, the pastor's visitation in the hospital should be as carefully planned as that of any other member of the healing team.

The pastor should not let his hospital visitation become stereotyped. Many times the chaplain of a hospital hears the remark, "My pastor was in to see me today but he was in such a hurry I did not talk to him about this matter." Certainly one would not deny the value of "pop" calls by the pastor, but it is plainly evident that unless the pastor's ministry has more depth than a cheery "Good morning," a wave of the hand, and an occasional prayer, the basic needs of many individuals are not being met. A wholesome balance must be maintained between this general ministry and the intensive ministry of the pastor in visiting the sick.

A pastor may have a noble ambition and a sincere desire, but it will be difficult for him to sustain the meaningful relationships of an intensive ministry to the sick if he overlooks the importance of note-writing and the keeping of records. Russell Dicks points out that note-writing contains four values: "It is a check upon one's work; it is a clarifying and developing process; it relieves emotional strain for the writer; the notes stand as a record of one's work." [33] Most ministers and hospital chaplains experience difficulty in making note-taking a definite part of their work. This is probably due to the fact that hardly anything reveals as much about one's own personality as an actual verbatim account of one's dealings with an individual in a life situation.

Note-taking furnishes concrete evidence of what actually takes place in a given situation. In any interpersonal relationship each person is reacting and being reacted upon, so that verbal expressions of attitudes and emotions are elicited. Such expressions, when examined objectively after the interview, will reveal much concerning both the patient and the pastor.

For example, the pastor may find characteristic faults of his own, such as the tendency to give reassurance too quickly, showing up in one interview after another. Unless he studies the verbatim accounts of more than one interview, he can go on making the same mistake indefinitely. Often the pastor will fail to realize the significance of some statement made by the patient in a face-to-face relationship, but when the total conversation is put down on paper, the same statement stands out like a red flag.

The following verbatim interview will serve to illustrate the above statements:

Patient: I can't see my folks near as much. My boy's too young to drive the truck down here. I'm afraid he'd wreck it and kill himself and the others, too. And since I got here I

---

[33] Richard C. Cabot, M.D., and Russell L. Dicks, *The Art of Ministering to the Sick* (New York: The Macmillan Company, 1945) p. 244.

found out I've got heart trouble. So, I've decided that I'm not driving no more cars and trucks.

Chaplain: You mean you're going to give up driving?

Patient: That's right. It's just too dangerous. Why, I might be driving the truck and have a wreck and *murder* my family.

(*Comment: The patient uses the word "murder" in connection with his own driving, but the word "kill" in reference to the son's driving. This turned out to be a significant slip of the tongue in this man's case. He had a terrific amount of hostility toward his wife.*)

Chaplain: Oh, I wouldn't worry too much about that. I know a man at home with heart trouble, and he never has stopped driving.

(*Comment: Here the counselor is giving reassurance without awareness of the man's problem, too fast and too early, as is indicated in the patient's reply.*)

Patient: Well, maybe so. (Pause) You know, this is a mighty big hospital. When I get out I want to visit over it.

While one is working with people day in and day out, it is almost impossible to carry the details of conversations in one's mind. Even the barest of notes listing the essential facts about the patient and the main topic of conversation can be of inestimable value in refreshing the memory just before the individual is visited again.

Notes should never be taken in front of the patient. This practice tends to prevent the patient from talking freely and also makes it harder for the pastor to give the person his full attention. The best practice for the beginner to follow is to write the notes immediately after a visit, so that the material can be recalled more easily. It is wise to begin by writing up a large number of short visits and attempting to recall every word spoken during the interview. With practice of this kind, it is almost unbelievable how nearly one can come to producing a verbatim account of a forty-five-minute session. This does not mean that the pastor will have time to write up all of his visits in detail. It does mean that he can improve his ministry to the sick by writing up some of his visits in detail just as writing out a sermon in full occasionally will improve his preaching ministry.

Since hospital visitation is an essential part of the healing ministry of the pastor, its methodology deserves a great deal of study. The importance of the initial contact with the patient cannot be stressed too strongly. One can render future visits useless by some blunder during the first visit. Illness is a frustrating experience, and the sick individual is therefore more likely to be sensitive, irritable, hostile, suspicious, and anxious than when in a state of health. For this reason the simplest sort of ill-timed movement can prevent the pastor from establishing a working relationship with the patient. In view of this fact the following simple rules, although they are mostly of a mechanical nature, should not be taken lightly as a guide to hospital visitation.

1. It is a good policy in general visiting not to go into any room where the door is closed without first finding out something of the circumstances that exist behind that door. Remember that most patients, unless they are asleep, critically ill, or highly nervous, like their door open or partly ajar after the morning bath. The nurse will be glad to furnish any necessary information, and the patient's family also may be helpful in this regard. Especially in the case of the critically ill patient, the pastor should get as much information as possible before seeing the patient.

2. Be very careful to note "No Visiting" and "Isolation" signs hanging on the door. These signs can be easily overlooked when the door is partially ajar. There is a definite reason for the "No Visiting" sign, of which the pastor should be aware. Even though it does not mean for him to keep out entirely when there is a good working relationship with the doctor, yet it will have a bearing upon the type of visit he makes. The "Isolation" sign denotes the

fact that the patient has a communicable disease. These patients suffer from severe loneliness because they are not allowed any visitors. The pastor should not overlook a parishioner of his during an experience of this nature, since his spiritual needs are likely to be even greater than those of most patients; but he should abide strictly by the regulations for precaution. The nurse will gladly help with supplying a mask and gown.

3. Look to see if the light is on over the patient's door, and if it is, do not enter at all until the nurse has taken care of the patient's needs. Even if the light is out and the door partly ajar, knock gently before entering the room. This is a simple rule, but many pastors carelessly overlook it at one time or another. The mistake is rarely made twice, however.

4. Do not touch the patient's bed. Watch for cords on the floor, apparatus such as a rack for holding intravenous fluid, and especially the crank handle on the foot of the bed. The following experience told by a patient will serve to show how sensitive sick people are to physical contact:

A few weeks ago it was necessary for me to enter our North Carolina Baptist Hospital to undergo a very delicate eye operation. After coming from the operating room I was instructed to lie flat on my back and not lift my head from the pillow since this would strain my eyes.

Lying there blindfolded for nearly three weeks I experienced many new sensations. I became acutely aware of voices, movements, and noises about me. But the one thing that stood out above everything else in my hospital experience was the number of times my bed was jarred, knocked, leaned against, and sat upon. After about a week of this, when I heard footsteps approaching I almost had a compulsion to yell out and say, "Please do not touch my bed!"

5. Size up the entire situation at a glance during the process of entering the room. By this means alone one can

determine to some extent what course the visit will take. Giving no indication of surveying the room, the pastor can notice the position of the patient in the bed, evidences of previous visitors (cards and flowers), special hospital equipment, and other indications of the patient's condition and outlook. If the patient is receiving intravenous infusions of blood or glucose, one's approach would not be the same as if the individual were sitting in a chair enjoying the last stages of convalescence.

6. Always let the patient take the lead in shaking hands. The pastor should not offer to shake hands unless the patient makes the first move in this direction. If the hand is extended, one should certainly take it, but should handle it gently, returning the pressure with like strength. This is no time to show one's athletic prowess!

7. Upon entering the room take a position, whether sitting or standing, in line with the patient's vision, so that the patient is not required to move around in the bed. If the patient is lying flat and the bed is not elevated, it is better to stand in a relaxed position. Stand at the side of the bed, since the height of a hospital bed makes it almost impossible for the patient to look one in the face without turning sideways.

8. Beware of letting the visit become a pathological conference. In other words, don't make a habit of sharing your own hospital experience or that of another with the patient. This is in reality "getting in bed with the patient." Many lay people seek to give consolation by telling the patient of someone else down the hall who is in a much worse condition. Even if the patient in question has only athlete's foot, while the person down the hall has had a leg amputated, he still has his painful itching and derives very little consolation from the knowledge of his neighbor's ill fortune.

9. Help the patient to relax. Experiments in relaxation

performed under the direction of Edmund Jacobson of the University of Chicago have yielded information that can be useful to the pastor in his work with the sick.[34] Doctor Jacobson's findings indicate that relaxation begins with the physiological processes before reaching the mind.[35] In extreme cases of nervous tension, good results have been achieved by making suggestions about "letting go" and relaxing, allowing the patient to practice relaxation for several minutes before a prayer is said in which words such as "deep settled peace," "calm," and "relaxation" are incorporated. Whether or not this method is used, the pastor, immediately upon entering the room of a patient, should seek to put the individual at ease as quickly and easily as possible.

In order to accomplish this aim, the pastor himself should be relaxed. Emotions are caught and absorbed through empathy. Therefore, quick, jerky movements or nervous habits, such as twirling a watch chain, should be avoided. One's approach and over-all manner should be such as to "give off" relaxation from one's person.

10. Do not carry emotional "germs" from one room to another. When one has listened to a sordid confession or dealt with any highly charged emotional situation, it is time well spent to go to the soda shop for a few minutes before going to the next patient. But it is even more helpful to spend a few seconds in prayer between visits. Only the grace of God and the pastor's love and understanding of people can remove some of the emotional effects upon the pastor as he visits in a general hospital.

11. Do not reveal negative emotional reactions through the voice, countenance, or manner. Often the patient will want to show the pastor his wound or a bottle of gallstones.

---

[34] Edmund Jacobson, *Progressive Relaxation* (Chicago: University of Chicago Press, 1929).

[35] Edmund Jacobson, *You Must Relax* (New York: McGraw-Hill, 1934).

Sometimes the patient may be in such a pitiful condition, or the odor in the room may be so disagreeable as to make the visit an unpleasant task. The nurses and doctors have to face this problem with the burned patient and other types of cases, and the pastor should school himself not to show his negative reactions in his countenance. Remember that the patient, if conscious, is humiliated about his own condition and aware of the burden he is placing upon others.

12. A pastor should not visit when he is sick. When one is not sick enough for bed, one is tempted to go on with the day's routine, especially with one's ministry to those patients facing crises. When one is sneezing and in the worst stage of a cold, however, one certainly should not be visiting the sick. If the pastor feels that he must make two or three calls in a hospital to fill a promise, he should secure a gauze mask from the nurse to cover his nose and mouth.

13. Do not make the visit too long. A pastor, of all people, should not be guilty of tiring the patient with long visits. Early visits to postoperative patients may last only a minute. The pastor may never let the patient speak, but simply says, "I just wanted to look in and let you know I am thinking about you. I will see you when you are feeling better." Visits involving counseling sessions, when the patient definitely wants to talk, should rarely exceed forty-five minutes.

14. "Don't whisper or speak in low tones to a nurse, to a member of the family or to anyone else in the sickroom or near it, if there is the slightest chance that the patient will see you or hear you." [36] Frequently members of the family of a critically ill patient are standing around the door of his room. The pastor should not only refrain from whispering to them, but should caution them against do-

[36] Cabot and Dicks, *op. cit.,* p. 26.

ing the same thing. Even though the patient is in a coma, the same rule applies. In one instance a doctor was the guilty party; the patient, although supposedly unconscious, heard every word spoken and was deeply hurt over what was said.

15. As a general rule, the pastor should leave when the patient's meal is delivered to his room. One might say, "Well! Your meal has arrived. Would you like for me to say grace for you before I go?" Often the patient is more interested in talking than eating at the moment and will insist that the pastor remain longer. But remember, the patient's attitude toward the pastor may change enormously fifteen minutes later while he is attempting to eat cold meat. Food and sleep are important factors in the recovery of a sick person, and the pastor's visits should not interfere with either.

16. When visiting a small ward, always make it a practice to speak to every patient present. If the pastor talks to one of the patients in a four-bed ward and then leaves immediately, the others are going to feel slighted. The patient visited is sure to say to the others, after the pastor leaves, "That was my pastor who came in to see me."

Beyond the mechanics of pastoral visitation lie the deeper levels of the interpersonal relationship established. Each patient has certain basic needs which the pastor must attempt to meet in his hospital ministry. The critically ill patient, for example, needs the companionship of his minister and a strengthened faith which will increase his will to live. In chronic illness the patient desires a genuine understanding of his plight; he needs to reach some sort of adjustment to the burden of the illness and to recognize the opportunities within the illness; he needs some hope and companionship; and he needs also to be assured that some bitterness and frustration are to be expected. What does the pastor bring to meet these needs—or more specifically, what are the pastor's resources for a hospital ministry?

1. The greatest resource at the pastor's command is the traditional role embodied in his own person. Christian literature abounds with statements concerning the power of the minister's influence among his people, but every minister has to experience its effect in an interpersonal relationship to realize a portion of its significance. Then there follows a humbling of oneself and the desire to become a servant. The hospital, possibly more than any other environment, affords an opportunity to observe this phenomenon at work.

The pastor's influence is not limited to his own personal appeal but is enhanced by a figurative power that is as old as religion itself. Patients place the pastor in all kinds of emotional roles. A wide variety of feelings and interpretations are called up in the initial contact with an individual. This reaction necessarily results from the symbolic nature of the pastor's role because it occurs, many times, before a good interpersonal relationship has been established.

John Rea Thomas published several years ago an interesting discussion of the patient's concept of the pastor's role, which may be summed up as follows: The pastor's first visit may precipitate resentment or suspicion, which represents probably a rebellion against religious authority. Such patients seem to think that the pastor has come around to check upon their behavior or church attendance. Other patients look upon the pastor as some sort of Santa Claus or "father" and expect him to answer all their questions and to remove all their fears and problems. Then there are people who feel that the pastor is a holy, otherworldly individual, who knows nothing about ordinary living; or there may be patients with hidden fears about

death who interpret his visit as a sign that they are seriously ill. Still others see in the pastor someone who can
help them work out a difficult emotional or spiritual problem.[37]

The following incident is an extreme example of a patient's reaction to the symbolic nature of the minister's
role. On his first visit to a patient who was being fed by
stomach tubes because of her inability to swallow solid
food, the chaplain prayed upon request. He remained with
the patient only about five minutes altogether. Before her
next meal, the patient asked the doctor to remove the
tubes, announcing that the chaplain had prayed for her
and she was healed. She ate the meal of solid food without
difficulty and went home the next day, reporting over the
community that she had been healed by the chaplain's
prayer.

Unless the pastor recognizes the significance of the symbolic nature of his role and the response it arouses in the
patient, he will fail to achieve a basic understanding of
the relationship established. This response is indicative
of the patient's attitudes toward God, the church, and his
own religious faith in general.

Rollo May calls this psychological phenomenon "empathy," which takes place in every interaction of personalities.

It is the feeling or the thinking of one personality into another until some state of identification is achieved. In this
identification real understanding between people can take
place; without it, in fact, no understanding is possible. It is
clear that the experience of empathy comes into every counselor's day dozens of times, whether it is recognized as such or
not.[38]

[37] John Rea Thomas, "Some Problems of Communication in the Bedside Ministry," *The Journal of Pastoral Care*, 4:3–4:2, Fall-Winter, 1950.
[38] Rollo May, *The Art of Counseling* (New York: Abingdon-Cokesbury
Press, 1939), p. 77.

According to May, then, the pastor's *own* responses that grow out of his conception of himself and his role as a minister would be equally as important as the patient's responses in the relationship established.

Carroll Wise has well said:

If God is thought of in terms of sentimental love, the pastor may work out his role by figuratively patting troubled people on the head and saying, "Don't worry. God will take care of it." If God is thought of and really felt to be redemptive love, seeking the fulfillment and redemption of each person, the clergyman will feel the necessity of expressing a similar attitude toward persons who seek help. But the pastor must examine himself here. Whatever his basic belief about himself as a minister, his role and function, these will be communicated to the troubled person, for good or for ill.[39]

Thus it becomes increasingly clear that the pastor's role as a representative of God occupies the central place in the healing methodology of his ministry to the sick. As Paul Johnson points out:

The resources of the pastor are greater than he knows— greater than his knowledge, his love, or his life. For the spirit creative that works in us and among us is more resourceful than we alone could be. The pastor's resources, though limited by his own limitations, are immeasurably enlarged by his relationships.[40]

2. Just as the pastor's role is grounded in tradition, so the Bible has traditionally been used by ministers to give reassurance and comfort to people whom they visit. The pastor in his hospital visitation will constantly use all of the spiritual tools at hand, and the Bible furnishes inexhaustible resources of strength and comfort for those who

---

[39] Carroll A. Wise, *Pastoral Counseling* (New York: Harper and Brothers, 1951), pp. 10–11.

[40] Paul E. Johnson, "The Pastor's Resources," *Pastoral Psychology*, 1:3:29, April 1950.

are facing crises in life. Like any other tool, however, it must be used with purpose if it is to be used effectively. Cabot and Dicks illustrate its use with lack of purpose in the following case:

A Jewish girl who knew little of religion and nothing of the Bible asked a minister for something to read which would help to maintain her courage through a difficult illness. The minister gave her a Bible saying, "Read this. Read anywhere in it. It's all good." [41]

In other cases the purpose may be inappropriate. For example, the minister who sat by a woman's bed and read one passage after another from the New Testament for forty-five minutes in an effort to convince her that she was saved was going to another extreme. This patient was depressed and obsessed with the idea of having committed the unpardonable sin. Her mind was in a feverish state, waiting to grasp any significant statement and read any meaning into it, but was blocked from receiving insight by logical thinking.

Possibly the best use that can be made of the Bible in hospital visitation is for the purpose of reassurance and comfort. In all cases, the selections should be brief, should be applicable to the situation, should be read well, and preferably should be familiar to the patient. Cabot and Dicks have discussed the use of the Scriptures to aid the patient in gaining perspective toward his illness.

Perspective is seeing life steadily and seeing it whole. . . . We can say to a patient who is suffering great pain, "Do not think about your pain." But he cannot follow such advice without perspective. . . . They need to see life steadily. They need to have called to their minds the stability of God. "I am thy rock and thy fortress." In such instances people do not want religion urged or lectured into them. They do not want

---

[41] Cabot and Dicks, *op. cit.*, p. 235.

it in the words of the minister but in terms they have always heard, terms which speak for themselves.[42]

Where there is a lack of religious background, but a seeking attitude, the Bible furnishes the most effective aid for giving the patient perspective, since one can almost always find in biblical literature an experience similar to one's own. Here the individual is led into a growth experience.

The pastor should commit to memory many of the great passages of the Bible that have brought comfort to Christians throughout the ages. Hospital chaplains have found invaluable the practice of quoting a verse or short passage of Scripture to the critically ill patient. During a visit with a certain patient who was facing an operation, the chaplain was asked to repeat several times, "Peace I leave with you; my peace I give to you; not as the world gives do I give to you. Let not your hearts be troubled, neither let them be afraid." [43] Three days later, just before the patient died, the chaplain placed his head inside the oxygen tent and repeated clearly and distinctly the same passage of Scripture. The patient roused out of a coma, opened her eyes, and looked up at the chaplain with recognition and a radiance upon her face that was unforgettable.

The pastor can often use the Bible to gain insight into the patient. One hears all kinds of interpretations of the Scriptures as one visits in a hospital. These interpretations, in many instances, reveal the deeper underlying needs of the personality to which one is ministering.

Regardless of the purpose for which the Bible or any other devotional literature is being used, it is always well to give the patient an opportunity to make some choice in the selection of the passages. This choice not only reveals something of the patient's attitudes, but assures the use

[42] Cabot and Dicks, *loc. cit.*, p. 235.
[43] John 14:27 (RSV)

of material that has familiarity and meaning from his past experience.

Occasionally the pastor will find it helpful to leave a verse of Scripture with a particular patient. The more the personal element can be brought into this ministry, the better; therefore, in the opinion of this writer, it is far more effective to write the verse down on a scratch pad or an old envelope that appears to be in the pocket by accident than to hand out printed material promiscuously in hospital visitation.

3. Prayer, intelligently employed is another potent therapeutic resource in the hospital ministry. Actually, the pastor should think of every face-to-face relationship with the patient as a form of prayer. He must constantly seek the mind of Christ, as made known through the presence of the Holy Spirit, in every interpersonal relationship established. Yet the pastor must know not only the mind of Christ, but also the needs of the sufferer, if prayer is to be used intelligently. This is even more important if the particular person involved does not recognize or accept prayer as a vital force in human experience.

As Charles Holman has said, "One weakness of religious ministry to sick souls has been that it has often sought to administer a spiritual panacea without adequate diagnosis of specific spiritual ills." [44] To avoid this error, the pastor does not use prayer as a part of every visit made to the sickroom. Unfortunately there is no "pat" formula which can be used to determine when one should pray. If a patient sends for the pastor, it can almost always be assumed that that individual would welcome prayer as a part of the visit. Further guidance must depend almost entirely upon intuitive judgment. An occasional prayer not specifically requested is far better than missing an opportunity where

---

[44] Charles T. Holman, *The Cure of Souls* (Chicago: The University of Chicago Press, 1932), p. 224.

prayer is desired but the patient is too timid to ask for it.

Prayer will be used by the pastor in his role as mediator during the ministry of confession. Often the patient's moral failure causes a sense of isolation, which so debilitates him that he becomes increasingly ineffective for good. Then, as Holman points out, "He needs someone to mediate between him and his beloved community, to bring to him once more the sense of its fellowship and aid." [45] Here the pastor leads the individual through the confession experience so that help is sought from God and the person is not left dependent upon the minister. Prayer then becomes a therapeutic resource for reintegration of life upon its highest levels—a goal which cannot be accomplished without religious motivations. A confessional prayer which lays the whole matter before God, when guilt has been suppressed, can be the best therapeutic and preventive agent the pastor has at his command.

Again, prayer will be used in the supportive ministry of the pastor. Here the pastor comes alongside those suffering acute physical pain, the chronically ill, the bereaved, the depressed, those facing an operation or adjusting to the loss of a limb through an amputation, and he calls to remembrance through intercessory prayer spiritual resources for comfort and encouragement.

Prayer also serves a teaching purpose as one ministers in the sickroom; that is, it teaches the patient to get beyond the immediate situation. Cabot and Dicks call this "reach" or "perspective" in prayer.

The following suggestions may be made concerning the use of prayer in the sickroom, when it is appropriate:

(1) A spirit of serenity and calmness within the pastor is essential. He should strive always for a mind open to the promptings of the Holy Spirit.

---

[45] *Ibid.*, p. 306.

(2) The prayer should be spoken in a conversational tone of voice.

(3) "The prayer should not be long—about the number of phrases that are contained in the twenty-third Psalm will be long enough." [46]

(4) Prayer should be used to lift the individual up to God and not for argument or exhortation.

(5) "It should recognize before God the essential spiritual need as recognized and understood by the parishioner himself." [47]

(6) "The parishioner himself should be helped to pray by clarifying in prayer, as explicitly as may be needed, the Christian attitude toward trouble and suffering." [48]

(7) "The form and content of a prayer should be consistent with the troubled parishioner's tradition and experience in the Christian life." [49]

(8) When a patient in a ward requests prayer, one can either call the other patients' attention to the fact that prayer is being offered and pray with the entire group before leaving the ward, or one may continue in the same conversational tone of voice and pray only with the individual. This choice will depend upon the circumstances existing in the ward at the time and the degree of personal attention required by the situation encountered.

(9) "The use of certain built-in passages of Scripture, which have been of mental aid for ages, stating with certitude the rightful expectation of the believer that all is well with him, is of more benefit than any home-made comfort devised on the spot." [50]

---

[46] Russell L. Dicks, *Pastoral Work and Personal Counseling*, revised edition (New York: The Macmillan Company, 1949), p. 186.

[47] Seward Hiltner, *Pastoral Counseling* (New York: Abingdon-Cokesbury Press, 1949), pp. 193–94.

[48] *Ibid.*

[49] *Ibid.* p. 194.

[50] Lloyd C. Douglas, *The Minister's Everyday Life* (New York: Charles Scribner's Sons, 1924), pp. 120–21.

4. If the pastor's "role" is disregarded, his ministry of listening will probably be the resource most frequently used in his hospital work. The advice to "listen" sounds so simple that many a minister has failed to recognize the value of this technique. I recall entering a patient's room one day, shortly after her pastor had left. Since I was well acquainted with her, she felt free to make this remark: "Do you know what the most irritating part of my hospital experience has been? It has been those people who have come into my room, trying to cheer me up by saying, 'Oh, you will be all right. We will see you out here on the street in a few days.' All the time I know the situation is serious." Her visitors should have been listening when they were talking. An effective ministry to any person requires some basic knowledge of the individual's need, and listening is the best-known method of finding out what the need is.

The fine art of listening is the most difficult technique to impart to the would-be counselor. Yet the heart of all counseling centers in the art of listening. Russell Dicks is right in saying that "if I were told I could have but one method in pastoral work, I would choose the listening method." [51] Dicks has probably made the greatest contribution to the literature dealing with this method of pastoral work. He points out that there are three conditions underlying listening: "Suffering on the part of the parishioner; rapport, which is probably the most important single factor in the healing, creative ministry of listening; and the stability and soul-poise of the listener." [52]

In describing it as a method, Dicks discusses four phases of the listening ministry: passive listening, active listening, interpretation, and reassurance.

Passive listening is characterized by a passive attitude on

[51] Russell L. Dicks, *Pastoral Work and Personal Counseling*, (New York: The Macmillan Company, 1945), p. 162.

[52] *Ibid.*, pp. 154–55.

the part of the pastor while the parishioner unfolds his story. Being passive, however, does not mean going to sleep. It means that the listener is relaxed, so as not to block the story by resistance, yet alert, nodding the head encouragingly and giving little grunts occasionally, until the surface stress is relieved. As the story unfolds, the parishioner's underlying behavior is discovered, and then a more aggressive type of listening may be required.

Active, or directed, listening includes asking questions, and the secret is to know what to ask—and when—as well as what not to ask. Through the use of questions, the individual's spiritual condition is explored, his suffering is relieved, new resources are released, insight is developed, and the counselor's interest in the person is expressed. When the relationship is strong enough, there is little danger of being too aggressive.

Interpretation is a phase of listening because without listening there would be nothing to interpret. Here the counselor interprets to the parishioner underlying behavior that the individual may not be aware of or may not understand. This method involves risks, however, as the pastor assumes that his interpretation is right and that the parishioner will accept it. It is a short-cut method, used primarily because of lack of time and because the active listening method has broken down.

Dicks names "reassurance" as the fourth phase of listening. He describes it separately because, like interpretation, it has little use apart from listening. It is characterized by a positive statement that the problem will work itself out or that the individual is able to overcome his suffering. The individual does not get courage simply by being told that he has it, but develops courage as one listens to him. As a method, reassurance should be used sparingly, and should be given in a simple language and in a voice and manner which reveal that it is sincere. It is given in the

name of the pastor and not in the name of the Trinity, as
Catholics give it. The advantage of this plan is that it
makes the reassurance intimate and personal, but its dis-
advantage is that the support of the Creator himself is lack-
ing.[53]

The pastor should use the resource of listening with
great care, sincerity, and deep sensitivity since it is a pow-
erful instrument for good or harm according to the skill
with which it is practiced. The degree of its use is completely determined by the depth of the relationship. On
routine visits the pastor has no ethical right to use any
technique that will cause the individual to reveal material
that he did not intend to share. Many times it is a temptation to "pull out," with the listening method, material one
knows is underneath, but nothing is ever gained by the
method unless the individual willingly enters into an experience of trusted sharing. On the contrary, hostility can
be aroused which will prevent any future relationship for
good. Many a theological student, with a reading knowledge of the literature on counseling, has entered clinical
work and lost relationship after relationship, until it was
pointed out to him that he was using listening as a method
of forcing material out too fast and thereby was straining
the relationship.

5. The use of the voice is so important in the sickroom
that it needs to be mentioned briefly as a definite resource
of the pastor. In the literature on the minister's resources,
hardly anything has been said in this connection. The voice
is closely connected with the pastor's role and also with the
empathy that takes place in the relationship; and an understanding of its use as a tool can lead to a more effective
ministry. There is probably nothing about a person which
will give away the inner state of his emotions more quickly

---

[53] *Ibid.*, pp. 155–62.

than the voice. Gray and Wise point out the effect of emotions upon the voice and discuss the quality and pitch of the voice in their relation to the feelings and attitudes within the individual.

> Psychologists are generally agreed that there is no such thing as a "pure idea" without its emotional aspect, its "effective tone," so to speak. If we think about things at all, we also feel about them. And while the words we are using may express precisely what we are thinking, they also have this personal, emotional meaning. . . .
>
> Quality is pre-eminently the characteristic having to do with attitudes, feelings, emotions; and in the portrayal of these attitudes the most profound variations are to be expressed by variations in the quality of the voice. . . .
>
> It is the extreme variations in pitch that reveal attitudes; but it might be pointed out that very narrow variations are, in a sense, as extreme as are very wide fluctuations, and hence have strong emotional significance.[54]

Even when one is relaxed and the voice is not charged with emotion, bad habits of enunciation or a nasal and rasping voice can get on other people's nerves and make the voice a negative element in empathy. When one is dealing with a highly emotional patient who talks in high-pitched tones, or praying with a cardiac patient who has an emotional religious background and whose life might be endangered if he became upset during a prayer, a calm, well-modulated voice is invaluable.

One should be consciously aware of the voice as a tool and should not follow the natural tendency to let the voice rise in speech or laughter until it equals the note of the person with whom one is talking, especially when that individual is somewhat overexcited. This caution is especially applicable in dealing with the hyperthyroid patient.

---

[54] Giles Wilkeson Gray and Claude Merton Wise, *The Bases of Speech* (New York: Harper and Brothers, 1934), pp. 307–308, 310.

The use of a calm, even tone of voice around a person who is talking in a high-pitched voice will produce a gradual change in the latter. This does not imply that one should assume an affected professional unctuousness or should go to the extreme of whispering, but it simply implies that one should consciously use the voice to create an atmosphere of peace and quiet.

Chapter Four

THE MINISTRY OF COUNSELING

Pastoral counseling as a resource for healing is embodied in the pastor's skill in caring for human problems in a face-to-face relationship. Three factors make counseling in a general hospital distinctively different from that ministry performed in the pastor's study. First, a pastor in the hospital must necessarily work in relation to other professional people who are legally responsible for the actual life of the patient. Second, the contact in the hospital is more brief than the contact in the study. Third, the environment of the bedside ministry is different.

In formal office counseling there is a frank recognition on the part of the individual of the existence of an emotional problem. If a pastor applies indiscriminately to the bedside ministry the techniques that would be appropriate in an office interview, his bedside ministry will not be effective. In the light of this major difference at the point of initial contact, it seems apparent that the pastor should meet the patient as near to his "growing edge" as possible and treat him as a responsible and emotionally healthy person until the evidence proves to the contrary.

The patient's average length of confinement in a general hospital is approximately seven days. A good relationship must be established immediately upon contact with the patient, and therapeutic efforts should proceed as rap-

74

idly and as intensively as the crisis situation warrants. The pastor must make appropriate adaptation of the techniques of counseling discovered by the psychotherapist. In line with Carl Rogers' presentation of nondirective counseling, I like to say that the pastor must be *directive in a nondirective manner.*

The specific role and function of the pastor as a therapeutic agent can be demonstrated best through a careful analysis of a series of actual verbatim interviews with the same person, revealing the complete pastoral relationship during the patient's stay in the hospital. Such a case history will have the added effect of laying bare a counseling relationship and of demonstrating a part of the method used in clinical training of theological students as taught by the hospital chaplain.

This material completely conceals the identity of the patient and the pastor in training. The latter is a graduate of Yale Divinity School and had used two of his summer vacations working as a pastor's assistant in a rather large church. After graduation from the seminary he spent two years as pastor of a church in an industrial area. Upon the advice of a medical doctor who was a member of his board of deacons, he secured a leave of absence from his church for a period of ten weeks. He came to the hospital for the stated purpose of "increasing his skill in ministering to the individual." It should be made clear in defense of the pastor that this case was written during the first three weeks of his clinical training before he had accumulated much reading knowledge in the field of counseling. In fact, the case written by a beginner was chosen deliberately in order that it might lend itself more readily to comment.

The student wrote these interviews from memory immediately after each contact with the patient, and they are presented just as they were written without any correction of style and sentence structure.

First Interview

The patient was a middle-aged lady. She was seated upon the side of the bed with a housecoat on and had just arrived at the hospital. She was in a four-bed ward.

Chaplain: I am John Doe, a minister with the chaplain's office. Your name is . . .

Patient: Mrs. Jones.

Chaplain: Where are you from, Mrs. Jones?

Patient: Bordertown.

(*Comment: The introduction could be improved upon. "My name is John Doe. I am a Baptist minister working here at the hospital with the chaplain. What is your name?" Then, "Well, it's nice to meet you. Where are you from, Mrs. Jones?" One's identity should be established clearly at the outset. Also, questions that are used should be those that are acceptable in any social relationship.*)

Chaplain: Your family there?

(*Comment: This question is too sharp and abrupt. "You are not far from home then. Do you have a family, Mrs. Jones?"*)

Patient: No, I don't have any family, just brothers and sisters.

Chaplain: You must have just come into the hospital. (Her suitcase was on the floor; she had on a housecoat, sitting up.)

(*Comment: If the chaplain had merely said, "Is that right?" or "Uh! uh!" the patient may have revealed more of her family situation, which would have been helpful for the counselor in later contacts.*)

Patient: Yes, I did, just got in. (Nurse came in to get patient ready for the doctor.)

Chaplain: It is nice to see you at first like this. I'll be coming back from time to time.

(*Comment: "It is nice to see you. If I can help you in any way while you are here please have the nurse to call me." This may have been better.*)

Patient: All right, come back. (Patient seemed nervous, kept rubbing hands together. This was taken to be a normal reaction from first coming into hospital.)

(*Comment: The patient had just arrived at the hospital and was obviously frightened as evidenced by short answers. The chaplain should have used this opportunity to welcome the patient into the hospital, put her at ease as much as possible, give her reassurance, offer his services, and then moved on.*)

Second Interview

Patient opened her eyes as I came up to the bed. I had talked briefly to two other ladies in the four-bed ward.

Chaplain: Looks like our talking has waked you.

(*Comment: The introduction should be repeated on the second visit. The patient is in a strange environment and meeting new people, and many of the doctors wear business suits.*)

Patient: No, I wasn't sleeping, just resting some. One of my eyes was hurting where it was hurt.

Chaplain: I saw you briefly yesterday when you were just coming in. Have you come to feel at home here?

Patient: More than that, I'm tired already. There is just nothing to do but lie here; the hours are too long. If I had something to do.

Chaplain: You told me you were from . . .

(*Comment: The chaplain could have said, "Have you always been very active?" or, he could have said, "The afternoons are long, are they not?"*)

Patient: Bordertown. I live with my invalid sister and mother there.

Chaplain: You didn't say that you worked there.

Patient: No, I don't work.

Chaplain: You just stay at home.

(*Comment: The chaplain is obviously not following the patient's lead, is not listening enough, and is more directive than he has a right to be in the hospital setting.*)

Patient: Well, you see I was married, but my husband ran off and left me. That was just a year ago last Thursday.

Chaplain: That must be tough.

(*Comment: The chaplain does not yet know enough about the problem to give intelligent sympathy. A nod of the head or "Is that right?" would have been sufficient at this point.*)

Patient: I never thought anything like that would happen to me.

Chaplain: And what was the trouble that . . . (I was going to ask about her illness.)

(*Comment: The chaplain is too directive. Also, why ask about her illness? That would have been a complete change of subject.*)

Patient: You mean between me and him? Well, . . .

Chaplain: I was just going to ask about the thing that brought you to the hospital.

(*Comment: The chaplain is running from the problem by changing the subject. One should rarely ask a female patient why she came into the hospital. And this individual will not make the mistake again as will be seen from the following answer given by the patient to the question above.*)

Patient: Oh, I have some discharge and some drainage up on that leg.

Chaplain: And you hope to get ready to go back home.

(*Comment: The chaplain became ill at ease after the patient presented her problem, which possibly accounts for his interjecting doubt concerning her recovery.*)

Patient: It's been pretty bad. I can't rest well.

Chaplain: Well, Mrs. Jones, I know that the thing you have told me has been terribly hard on you.

Patient: Yes, it has. I want you to pray for him, as well as me. He left and never came back. He didn't leave me but $50.00 to my name. That was one thing that made it so hard on me. We had $12,000. If he had even told me about it and split evenly. When they found them they were in another state. He was sending her children to school. That woman has a husband living, too. He is in another town. She has four children, but she is younger than I am; she's only thirty. They had been out west and all around. Now he is in Brown City, I guess. I don't hear from him any more. He told me he was through with me, so I don't bother him. I just let him go.

Chaplain: I know this has been harder on you than I can imagine.

Patient: It was mighty hard. I came to stay with my sister. She is a widow, and she keeps my mother and an invalid sister. So I stay with them. They thought I would have a nervous breakdown over it, but I didn't. We don't see why things happen, but the Lord has a reason for all things. In the long run they will work out for the best.

Chaplain: I will be coming back to see you, Mrs. Jones; sometimes it helps a lot to talk about the tough things that happen to us.

Patient: I don't bother people with it. I just try to go on and bear it myself. People don't want to listen to your troubles; they don't understand. I never understood how to sympathize with a person like that before. But I do now.

Chaplain: But if someone can understand there might be a lot of help for all of us when these things happen to us. You have probably already seen that it is hard to stay physically and spiritually healthy with too much of a burden on us.

(*Comment: The chaplain has clarified his relationship nicely here.*)

Patient: Yes, it is. (Nurse came into the room.)
Chaplain: I'll undoubtedly see you tomorrow, Mrs. Jones.

(*Comment: The patient obviously wanted to tell someone about her problem and was ready to talk in this interview. The chaplain came very near blocking her feelings by changing the subject, but the pressure caused the patient to talk in spite of his blunder. Nevertheless, the chaplain has a good relationship established for future interviews. A better statement with which to end the visit would have been, "Mrs. Jones, I certainly appreciate your sharing these confidences with me and I shall be praying for you during your stay here in the hospital. I will see you again tomorrow and we can talk some more about these questions." A prayer for strength and under-*

standing would have been quite appropriate at the end of the interview. It would have released energy and strengthened rapport.)

Third Interview

I saw her doctor after the last visit and the following information came from him. "Patient married about twenty-six years, no children. For fifteen years troubled with unusual secretions near genital region. Evidence of long standing trouble there, operation contemplated. He did not know why she came at this time to the hospital, why she had not done something years before. Patient had been examined once by doctor, treatment temporary, she never went back."

Patient was seated in a chair looking at a magazine when I entered the room.

Chaplain: I see you are reading.

Patient: No, I was just looking. I just don't have anything to do. It wouldn't be so bad if I had something to do.

Chaplain: They don't make you stay in bed? (Another patient was sitting close by listening.)

Patient: No, they let me run around.

Chaplain: You are getting along well, then?

Patient: Yes, I feel all right. (Nurse came by and stuck a chart under mattress.) (*Nurse:* "The doctor will be by in a little bit.")

Patient: More doctors. They brought a lot of them to look at me. They haven't seen a case like mine.

(*Comment: The patient sounds as though she might be deriving some satisfaction from this state of affairs.*)

Chaplain: I suppose you told the doctors things you told me.

Patient: Yes, he asked me and I told him about it.

Chaplain: You told him how long you had this condition?

(*Comment: Here the chaplain is using the information listed at the beginning of this interview which he had received from the doctor. Information obtained from other sources should rarely be brought into an interview, especially in situations of this nature. This raises a real issue as to the worth-*

whileness of having too much information from doctors and from the chart. It does prejudice the interview.)

Patient: Yes, fifteen years.

Chaplain: A long time.

Patient: Yes, my sister told me to come; she is the one who got me to come. She said that I could get well of this and be able to work.

Chaplain: Your sister tries to understand you?

(*Comment: Naturally the patient will agree with this question. In the first place it presupposes the answer, and in the second place if there was hostility here it is too early for it to come out.*)

Patient: Yes, she is a lot of help. Her husband is dead.

Chaplain: Your mother, how does she feel toward you?

(*Comment: The chaplain has no right to ask such questions. The patient has been talking freely and the chaplain should be listening and using every technique to appear to be talking when he is not.*)

Patient: She is good to me—tries to keep me from worrying about it. They both have meant a lot to me.

Chaplain: I can imagine that they have.

Patient: I was almost a nervous wreck last year. But me and another girl did some work that helped me. You know where _____ town is? There was a small church there. I always like to do the Lord's work, helping people. My husband and I did the Lord's work ten years.

(*Comment: Two causes have become evident that are responsible for the marriage breakup, namely, the physical difficulty of the patient and the competition existing between the couple in their work.*)

Chaplain: You just started out . . .

Patient: We went to school two years first.

Chaplain: In?

Patient: We worked as we went to school. I've always enjoyed doing the Lord's work; it helps you so much. It takes your mind off yourself, your own problems.

Chaplain: You mentioned before that you had seen some

personal problems of other people as you went around. Did people talk to you about some of these?

(Comment: It might have been better to have said, "You had problems at that time?" The chaplain had a legitimate right to respond to material brought out by the patient of her own accord.)

Patient: Yes. Like a man running off with another woman, or a woman wanting to live for the Lord and the man not caring and not wanting to live right.

Chaplain: You mean you tried to think of other people's troubles and happiness before you considered your own.

Patient: Yes, I did.

Chaplain: Did you consider that it had to be either their happiness or yours, couldn't it be both?

(Comment: The chaplain attempts interpretation, but it is too early, as can be seen from the following answer by the patient. She needs to reveal a great deal more before she will be able to gain real insight into herself. Yet the chaplain is under the pressure of time and a new situation himself.)

Patient: Well, I have always thought of the other person. My husband, I always tried to be good to him. Many people in the community told me that I tried to be too good to him, and that is one reason he left.

Chaplain: Too good?

Patient: Yes.

Chaplain: Things like . . .

Patient: Like keeping the house right, taking care of him, helping in his life.

Chaplain: In his work?

Patient: Yes, in his work. But he was always the kind that thought he was a little better than me, and knew more than me. I had to always take the *bottom part.*

Chaplain: The bottom part?

Patient: Yes. When we were going to do something, or when we were planning something . . . (A couple of nurses came in to work on patient in other bed. Too much noise, not private enough to talk.)

Patient: I have pretty good control of myself. I have myself under subjection. The doctor says I am not so nervous now. The Lord says to cast our burden on him, and that is what I have tried to do.

Chaplain: Yet it is mighty hard sometimes.

(*Comment: The chaplain is somewhat panicked by the nurses and is letting them run him out of the ward too fast. He meant to give sympathy but was too brief in what he had to say. A prayer with the patient at this point would have probably deepened the relationship.*)

Patient: Yes, it is hard.

Chaplain: I'm going to be coming back, Mrs. Jones.

Patient: You can be praying for me. It is good to talk to you.

(*Comment: The chaplain was working under difficult circumstances in this interview. Another patient was sitting near by at the beginning of the contact and there were two interruptions by the nurse. However, he has the confidence of the patient in spite of seeming to be too aggressive at times, and he followed the patient's leads better than he did in the second interview, but he still needs to improve on the creative listening technique.*)

Fourth Interview

Patient had asked me in a brief visit the day before to see what happened to a lady who was in the ward with her.

Chaplain: I can't find what happened to Mrs. _____. She is not in the hospital.

Patient: I'm sure they took her home Sunday. Some of her people came in and told me.

Chaplain: How is it with you?

Patient: Oh, I'm going home tomorrow.

Chaplain: You are?

Patient: Yes, I've got along fine; the Lord has certainly been with me.

Chaplain: Well, fine.

Patient: After I get well, I can work and be independent.

Chaplain: You want to be independent?

Patient: Not really. But I don't want someone to have to

keep me up and pay my bills. Everybody wants to do that, don't you think?

Chaplain: You mean everybody wants to be independent enough not to be a burden.

Patient: Yes, that's right.

Chaplain: Well, I certainly hope you work out a happy life at home. I wanted to see you more, but you know how busy this ward is.

Patient: It has been good knowing you. Have you ever lived in _____?

Chaplain: No, I have just been through a number of times.

Patient: I was raised there. We lived there all the time before my husband was saved.

Chaplain: You mean you lived there before your husband became a Christian.

Patient: Yes. We have been saved twelve years. (Pause) Of course we went to school, then traveled in the Lord's work. Are you any kin to the _____ in _____?

Chaplain: No, I'm sure. I had a sister who used to live near there.

Patient: I know a man there by your name. He is pretty wealthy.

Chaplain: I suppose he couldn't be any kin of mine then. (Pause) Mrs. Jones, I know telling the things you have told me must still be painful. These very tough things happen to us and . . .

Patient: Yes, it is pretty bad. But all I can do is forget it, and turn him over to the Lord.

Chaplain: Forget it?

(*Comment: Here the chaplain was attempting to keep the patient in contact with reality in order that she might adjust to the problem rather than use the unhealthy mechanism of repression. It would have been less abrupt to have said, "But we don't really forget such experiences as you have had. Isn't it more a matter of learning how to live with the experience and asking God to help us?"*)

Patient: Well, I can't really forget it, but I have to try to do the best I can. It won't do me any good or him either to try not to give him up. Worry won't help anybody, will it?

Chaplain: You mean we have to live with people, in spite of the rough things.

Patient: Yes, I just have to keep it out of my mind and get the Lord's help.

Chaplain: You said you couldn't really forget . . .

Patient: No, I will never really forget him. They arrested him for living in adultery. I went and saw him in jail. He has to admit that I was a good wife.

Chaplain: A good wife?

Patient: Yes, I feel I did my best. I told him, "I gave you the best years of my life." And he said so, too. He said he knew I loved him. He didn't doubt that.

Chaplain: You feel that you have done your best.

Patient: Yes, I did all I could for him. I went because I thought I could go and give him a last chance if he wanted to make up and do things right. At least he couldn't say that I hadn't done all I could, and my soul would be right with God. He said he was through with me. Told me to go ahead and do as I pleased, told me to go on and get someone else and marry. He said, "I've ruined both of our lives."

Chaplain: I can imagine.

Patient: But I told him there would never be another one, and he said he knew it. We got married when we were young; he was _____ and I was _____. My father was against it.

Chaplain: Your father was against it?

Patient: Yes, we were so young.

Chaplain: I have heard that if people are prepared for marriage and are somewhat mature it will take three to five years for the kind of adjustment that is really wholesome. It is not an easy job.

Patient: No, it isn't.

Chaplain: Many times we can't understand our actions or see any reason for them. But when we are born into the world, certain things influence us in this or that direction. There is a reason for our actions; we don't just do things. We haven't mentioned reasons for your husband's action.

Patient: I don't understand it.

Chaplain: I'm sure that it is hard to understand. But do you see that there might be reasons. You see, I know you are going home. You have a job ahead. You may be able to understand yourself and your past enough to really help. I'm only here to try to help you. I wonder whether you had in your mind connected your trouble, the condition that brought you here, if you had connected that with your husband's action, finally leaving.

(Comment: The chaplain is aware that this patient is going home and obviously feels a compulsion to get her problem solved. Fortunately for the patient she cannot see what the chaplain is trying to interpret. If she could see the whole truth about her marital breakup she would really need help. The counselor should stay alongside the individual as he works through his problem and never get out too far in front. This paragraph reveals cross-currents of emotion within the chaplain himself.)

Patient: Well, no. He never did think I should go to a doctor.

Chaplain: He didn't?

Patient: No, he thought I would be all right. It didn't bother me so much then, so we just kept putting it off.

Chaplain: You don't have reasons in mind then?

Patient: Well, my husband was running around with women before we were saved.

Chaplain: You mean in the earlier part of marriage?

Patient: Yes, after about one year he started. But he never treated me bad, not even then. He respected me.

Chaplain: Respected you?

Patient: Yes, he never came home drunk. If he got drunk he would wait till he was sober.

Chaplain: You feel that he cared for you then?

Patient: Yes, he did.

Chaplain: The other parts of your marital relationship; do you consider that they were what you might call wholesome or about normal?

Patient: Well, yes. When he bought me anything, he would

want me to have the best. He didn't just buy anything for me. It was all right till about three years before he left. He didn't treat me too bad, but I could tell there was a difference.

Chaplain: It is certainly hard to understand.

Patient: Well, he just got in with this woman, I guess.

Chaplain: You think that is all.

Patient: I weighed 160 pounds, and she only weighed 110. (Pause)

Chaplain: You feel weight had something to do with it?

Patient: Well, but he weighed 206. He was a big man. I think now that that woman almost forced herself on him, too. And he liked babies, and we never had any.

Chaplain: He liked children?

Patient: Yes, we wanted some.

Chaplain: You wondered about that—were you ever examined?

Patient: No. He would say, well, maybe children would be in the way of our work, so let's just wait and not worry about it.

Chaplain: Did the doctors say anything about it this time?

Patient: No, only that nothing was wrong there, and that they could see no reason why I didn't have any.

Chaplain: Yes, it could be a number of things on both sides. These things can be pushed down, but not forgotten, like you said.

Patient: I know it does good to get them out.

Chaplain: Yes, something this tough may need to be discussed with a doctor, a preacher, one of the family, or someone every once in a while.

Patient: But you can't discuss them with everyone. So many don't understand. It's hard to find someone who understands.

Chaplain: Yes, the person must try to understand. I'm going to have to leave, but I'll try to see you before you go home. I have faith along with you to believe that God can help you and that you can live a happy life.

Patient: He will help me all right. The thing I most want to do is to work and help in the church, get people in the church, help them to be saved and all. (Pause)

Chaplain: I wonder why that is.

Patient: I just like that kind of work.

Chaplain: Do you remember that I said people just don't do things right off the bat? And you told me about wanting to help others all the time.

Patient: Yes, I want to help other people. It keeps your mind off yourself.

Chaplain: Have you ever thought that God gave us a healthy amount of selfishness. You told me that some people told you you were not selfish enough.

Patient: They did tell me that many times. But I always disliked selfish people. But I don't think there is any danger of my being too selfish.

Chaplain: I doubt it myself. Have you ever watched children play. You see the child over in the corner when some children are playing ring around the rosy or something like that. You talk to him and he will say that he doesn't like to play or he doesn't even want to play such a silly thing. In truth we know that he wants to enjoy himself like the others. But he feels that . . . (Nurse came in, stuck thermometer in her mouth, stood there.) I will try to see you before you leave. I'd better go now. (She waved good-by.)

(*Comment: The chaplain used too much of a question and answer method in this entire interview, which is to guide the mind of the individual rather than letting the process of association take place. This individual would talk freely if the chaplain would only listen. Yet, one must agree that the probing has not broken the relationship. Rapport has deepened with each contact.*)

Fifth Interview

Spoke briefly to three ladies in the room, then walked over to bed of Mrs. Jones. I knew she was supposed to leave hospital.

Chaplain: You are not gone yet?

Patient: No, I'm patiently waiting. It takes an hour and a half for them to drive over. (Pause)

Chaplain: It has been nice to see you while you have been here.

Patient: I have enjoyed talking to you also. I've appreciated your prayers and I want you to keep praying for me.

Chaplain: We can have a prayer before you go today. As you go home you have a job, hope to build a wholesome life in many ways. Some plans, even selfish ones . . . (Smiling)

Patient: (She laughed.) You think I ought to be selfish?

Chaplain: What do you think about it?

Patient: Well, with all that has happened to me I guess I can afford to be.

Chaplain: Do you remember, Mrs. Jones, that we were talking about reasons for our doing things?

Patient: Reasons for being selfish?

Chaplain: And reasons for being very, very unselfish. (She laughed again, and yet the relationship was sort of serious, too.) Do you remember that we were talking about children playing when we were interrupted?

Patient: Yes, I remember.

Chaplain: The child standing off, not enjoying himself. I was wondering whether you see what I mean.

Patient: Well . . . (She looked puzzled.) (Long pause)

Chaplain: Like the child, if we are not happy and enjoying our lives we might say, "Well, I'll take it out in working in church and helping others."

(*Comment: The chaplain has realized since the last interview that he must lower his goal in what he attempts to accomplish in this short-term relationship. This interview illustrates the teaching element that has a place in pastoral counseling, especially when time is a limiting factor. The chaplain uses the parable method, however, rather than the telling method of giving advice, which has the advantage of letting the individual take the initiative in his own growth.*)

Patient: Oh, I don't plan to spend all my time in church.

Chaplain: Don't plan to spend all your time in church?

Patient: No, I can do other things, too.

Chaplain: Other things?

Patient: I can go on a vacation sometimes and do other things.

Chaplain: Vacation?

Patient: Yes, to the mountains or somewhere. Don't you think that will be good?

Chaplain: What do you think?

Patient: I think I can do that and serve the Lord, too.

Chaplain: And the other things?

Patient: Well, I can go hiking some. (Laughing) I like to go hiking very much. And I like to cook. (She mentioned a couple other things.) I can do these things and still serve the Lord.

Chaplain: You are giving yourself this advice?

Patient: Yes, I think I am. (Smiling)

Chaplain: I must say that I think you are giving yourself some very good advice. I believe that God meant for us to be happy, and then we can serve and bring others to him even better.

Patient: You know, I think so, too. (Pause)

Chaplain: If you would like to have prayer now, we can do that. (At that time two ladies came into the room.) This must be your folks coming after you. (Patient's mother and friend came in, mother embraced her.)

Patient: This is my mother and Mrs. _____, a friend from home. This is Preacher _____. He was just going to have a prayer with me.

Chaplain: (Prayer) Our Father, we are thankful for more blessings than we could name. Especially for our Saviour and for his Spirit who goes with us in all the tough places of life. Go with this servant who goes back to her home. May thy Spirit lead her, giving her strength and courage to build a wholesome and joyful life in the service of thy Kingdom. Amen.

Patient: (Asked me to come to see them.) (Thanked her, said good-by to all in room.)

Composite Criticism

1. The chaplain used a rationalistic approach rather

than that of letting the patient relive her experience emotionally in a warm sympathetic atmosphere. For example, "We haven't mentioned reasons for your husband's action," a statement which appears in the fourth interview.

2. In the total pastoral relationship the chaplain attempted to saddle the patient with ethical concepts far beyond her maturity and psychological ability to understand, much less to appropriate into her way of life. This fact appears specifically in the fifth interview when the chaplain remarked, "Like the child, if we are not happy and enjoying our lives we might say, I'll take it out in working in church and helping others."

3. This patient never really talked off the surface-exterior of her personality for her real self to become apparent either to herself or to the counselor. He tried to get information from her rather than to attempt to create a spiritual climate that would melt the barriers within herself and between her and him. He got in the way as her real self began to emerge.

What type of ministry should have been attempted under the rigid limitations of a hospital situation? Or, in other words, what were some of the patient's basic emotional needs?

1. There were situational fears that needed to be relieved. The patient was nervous in the initial visit, probably a reaction to the hospital environment. A further evidence of fear is the fact that the individual had not gone to a doctor for treatment but one time in fifteen years.

2. The individual made an appeal for *understanding* and not for *exhortation*. She mentioned three times during the interview other people's understanding her.

3. The problem of loneliness was a real factor in this woman's situation. She had no visitors during her hospital experience.

4. The fact that she did not react strongly to the chap-

lain's role as a minister reflects a superficiality in her religious experience. It would seem like a natural response for a woman who had had a preacher-husband to run off and leave her to have felt hostile toward another minister.

5. However, the real crux of the entire problem, from the chaplain's point of view, was one of *bereavement*. This patient was shocked and bereaved over the loss of her husband and at the same time had mixed feelings toward herself, as evidenced by her visit to the jail, which was probably one last effort to rid herself of any blame. Also, her self-esteem had been shattered and she was facing an inevitable life situation.

Nevertheless, the chaplain did furnish the individual with a certain amount of support. He prayed with her, listened some, but most of all he was faithful to her by paying her a visit each day that she was in the hospital. He probably supplied her with more understanding than she had ever known from any person outside her family. Even though he missed the immediate and obvious needs in many instances, and raised the more remote and obscure difficulties in others, this criticism is not to say that the total pastoral relationship was not vitally important to the patient in her hospital experience.

Chapter Five

THE SPECIFIC MINISTRY
OF THE PASTOR

The hospital as an institution in society has various connotations for different individuals. There was a time when being taken to a hospital meant that death was frightfully near. This idea carries over in many instances to the present day. Especially is this true of individuals who come out of rural areas. Regardless of the changing attitude toward hospitalization, the hospital to most people is a strange environment, characterized by unaccustomed routines, unusual odors, new people, needles, uncertainty, anxiety, and concentrated suffering.

Over and above the natural anxiety associated with the hospital experience—an anxiety which all the personnel in the institution should strive to reduce—there are certain crucial periods, crises, and major adjustments going on twenty-fours a day in the lives of various patients. The pastor should be aware of these critical opportunities with individuals who are facing an operation or death, with the bereaved, with the physically handicapped, and with the chronically ill. Certainly much progress has been made, through the use of sedation and anesthesia, in keeping physical pain at a minimum; but there is as yet no hypodermic devised that can be injected into a man's soul to lessen the pain of the spirit. The ministry to the soul is the heart of the pastor's task.

Ministering to the Surgical Patient

The thought of facing surgery produces a measure of shock in any mature person. As Cabot and Dicks have wisely pointed out,

The preparation of one's mind to face a surgical operation is a task to which too little attention is given. . . . The average man has not the remotest conception what surgical treatment involves, the reasons for pre-operative or post-operative procedure, or what he is to expect in the operating room.[55]

Yet Weiss and English say that surgeons do very little for the patient's state of mind:

Surgeons are always so careful to prepare their patients physically for operations. They would not think of performing a major operation without knowing that the cardiovascular-renal system had been surveyed, but they almost never give any consideration to the personality of the patient: how much anxiety is present, and what the effects of a surgical experience may be as far as the personality is concerned.[56]

Each type of surgical operation is associated with a different emotional response. An eye operation will serve to illustrate the need of a definite ministry by the pastor to the surgical patient.

The patient who is admitted to the hospital for eye surgery must not only cope with the physical distress which he already feels, he also knows that he is to have an operation which may cause severe pain when he recovers from the anesthesia. He knows that he must remain in the hospital for an indefinite period of time, and that he must exist in total or partial darkness with the outcome of the operation in doubt until the

---

[55] Richard C. Cabot, M.D., and Russell L. Dicks, *The Art of Ministering to the Sick* (New York: The Macmillan Company, 1944), p. 283.

[56] Edward Weiss and Spurgeon English, *Psychosomatic Medicine,* second edition (Philadelphia: W. B. Saunders Company, 1949), p. 728.

bandages can be removed and his eye, or eyes, tested. What does tomorrow really hold for him? [57]

Regardless of what the surgeon does for the mind of the patient during his operative experience, the pastor may not invade certain aspects of the situation. Allen S. Johnson says that the four questions which are most often asked the doctor by the surgical patient are: "Is it serious? Is the operation dangerous? Will I get well? Am I going to die?" [58] Such questions as these are totally in the realm of the medical profession, and the pastor should always refer them to the patient's doctor.

Preoperatively as well as postoperatively, however, there is an area where the pastor should not fail to minister. In the preoperative period, the patient's anxieties are likely to deal with unknown and unpredictable situations. Here, fear is the basic enemy that the mind has to encounter. The effects of fear in the preoperative period are pointed out by Harmer and Henderson:

No matter what seems apparent from the patient's attitude, every medical worker should realize that some degree of fear probably exists. All efforts are directed toward lessening the friction and the apprehension experienced by the patient. The injurious effects of fear on the nervous system are referred to in many places in this book. Pre-operatively, fear may produce effects violent enough to make the administration of the anesthetic difficult and to contribute to the factors producing shock.[59]

Some of the fears to which the pastor should minister in the preoperative patient are:

---

[57] Olga M. Weiss, "Psychological Aspects of Nursing Care for Eye Patients," *American Journal of Nursing*, April, 1950, p. 219.

[58] Allen S. Johnson, "The Physician-Patient Relationship," *The Journal of Pastoral Care*, 3:31:3–4, (Fall-Winter), 1949.

[59] Bertha Harmer and Virginia Henderson, *Textbook of the Principles and Practice of Nursing*, fourth edition, revised (New York: The Macmillan Company, 1946), pp. 805–806.

1. Fear based upon ignorance. This type of fear may be related to ignorance concerning some simple technique or procedure connected with preparing the patient for operation. Every pastor will meet this sort of fear, which can usually be alleviated with a brief explanation. An example is found in the individual who becomes upset through lack of understanding when his wife is called in to sign papers permitting an operation.

2. Fear connected with uncertainty, the unknown, or the possibility of death. Cabot and Dicks have said that "there are few adult patients who go to the operating room without thinking of the possibility that they will die during or soon after the operation." [60]

3. Fear based upon coming adjustments that must necessarily follow the operation. Many people who undergo an operation are fully aware that it means facing life debilitated or completely handicapped. More attention is given this problem in a later section on ministry to the handicapped.

4. Fear resulting from the necessity for a waiting period before the operation can be performed. This type of fear is seen in the patient's waiting to hear the verdict of the doctor as to whether a test revealed cancer. Anxiety, impatience, and fear tend to mount during the waiting period.

5. Fear connected with taking the anesthetic. Many patients do not realize that they will be given sedation before going to the operating room, and a simple stating of this fact may help many individuals to overcome this fear.

The ministry of the pastor to the preoperative patient is largely one of support. The pastor should use every resource at his command in giving comfort and encouragement to the patient. The most effective method of support,

---

[60] Cabot and Dicks, *op. cit.*, p. 288.

however, is probably the listening ministry, which helps the individual to bring his apprehension out into the open and to work out a philosophy toward it. To aid the patient in doing this, after a friendly relationship has been established, it is a good idea to ask how he feels about the coming operation. I have yet to ask a question of this nature when the patient did not seem to welcome an opportunity to express himself.

The preoperative patient probably offers the best opportunity for the pastor to reinforce the patient's faith in the doctor. In many instances, the individual is referred to a medical center by his local doctor and does not know the surgeon who is to operate on him. In such cases the patient can be greatly encouraged by a simple statement, when it can be made in sincerity, such as, "You certainly have a good doctor. I have known him for several years and have a great deal of confidence in his ability."

Clinical experience indicates that probably the most vital phase of the pastor's ministry to the preoperative patient is the influence it has in strengthening the individual's will to live and the quieting effect which religious resources can have upon the total organism. The patient's mental attitude toward his illness has a great deal to do with his chances of recovery. Many physicians will testify that some individuals die, when, according to medical science, they have a good opportunity to recover, while others live with apparently insurmountable odds to overcome. Thus, if the pastor can supply courage and faith to strengthen the patient's will to live, he may have contributed a deciding factor.

The patient's problems in the immediate postoperative period, before long-range adjustments come into focus, are concerned chiefly with his present discomfort or with unpleasant incidents connected with his treatment. His sole concern in the beginning may be that of existing. While fighting for his life, he may experience nausea, receive intravenous infusions in the arm, be encased in an oxygen tent, or be weighted down with appliances to maintain traction on a leg or an arm. In the midst of such discomfort, his span of attention is narrowed more or less to the immediate circumstance.

The pastor's ministry to the postoperative patient, especially during the first few days after the experience, is almost wholly dependent upon the relationship established before the operation. This ministry is largely that of standing by and is carried out through short, frequent visits. It is a relationship of going alongside, through the valley of suffering, giving strength and encouragement.

As the postoperative experience moves from the period of extreme discomfort to the somewhat brighter, yet confining, stages of convalescence, the patient becomes more concerned about future adjustments. The resource of counseling, discussed in chapter four, may now be used to a greater degree.

Ministering to the Convalescent

The rehabilitation of the twenty-three million disabled people in this country is a major medical problem having definite implications for pastors.[61] Every general hospital has its share of these disabled people in various stages of convalescence. The postoperative patient is handicapped, when, because of pain or difficulty in moving about, he is unable to perform the daily activities related to self-care. The medical patient weakened by months of debilitating illness is unable to dress, feed himself, or walk. The neurological patient is even more dependent on others to help him with the simple requirements of daily living. The patient in an iron lung or in a cast is another one of the

---

[61] Alice B. Morrisey, R.N., "The Nursing Technics in Rehabilitation," *American Journal of Nursing*, September 1949, p. 545.

many handicapped persons who face difficult psychological problems of adjustment.

Menninger has emphasized the psychiatric aspects of rehabilitation.

A major aspect of physical rehabilitation is the personality readjustment. When Doctor Rusk started the convalescent hospitals in the Air Forces, it was presumed that the chief job was a rehabilitation of a physical function. As time went on in these hospitals as well as the Army Service Forces Hospitals, psychiatric aspects of the job assumed primary importance. Psychiatry came to play a leading role in every one of these hospitals.[62]

Menninger's opinion has been corroborated by Strecker, who is quoted as saying:

It is not an overstatement to say that fully fifty per cent of the problems of the acute stages of an illness and seventy-five per cent of the difficulties of convalescence have their primary origin not in the body, but in the mind of the patient.[63]

Numerous physicians have expressed the belief that failure to recognize the psychic factor in illness, or to handle it properly, is responsible for the fact that many patients never make a complete recovery from an illness or operation, even where there is no evidence of organic illness remaining.

There are too many patients today who, already well on their way to an excellent recovery, suddenly and unaccountably develop what we are coming to call the "chronic invalid reaction" and never quite recover.[64]

---

[62] William C. Menninger, *Psychiatry in a Troubled World* (New York: The Macmillan Company, 1948), p. 436.

[63] Quoted by Flanders Dunbar, "Problems of Convalescence and Chronic Illness," *American Journal of Psychiatry*, 92:1095, 1936.

[64] Flanders Dunbar, "The Psychic Component of the Disease Process (Including Convalescence) in Cardiac, Diabetic, and Fracture Patients," Part II, *American Journal of Psychiatry*, 95:1319, 1939.

According to Dunbar, patients are often found lying side by side with the same illness, being apparently of the same general constitutional type, but still making quite different types of recovery.

Thus it becomes increasingly clear that the degree of discomfort and disability which the sick person suffers depends not only upon the severity of the illness, but also upon the meaning which the illness has for that individual at that particular time. This interaction between mental attitudes and physical well-being adds more responsibility for those who work with the convalescent patient.

Convalescent patients in a general hospital fall into three groups: (1) those who have been through an acute illness but will return to normal; (2) those who recover from their illness but are left physically handicapped; and (3) those who face a future in which they can expect only an increased amount of pain and disability, as in certain cases of arthritis or cancer. Patients in this last group are usually in and out of the hospital during the rest of their lives.

The pastor should seek to understand the basic problems inherent in convalescence, since the tenaciousness of the patient's hold on life may be of primary importance in a crisis. What are some of these problems?

First of all, the patient's attitude toward his illness may be a problem. One individual may tend to give up in the face of obstacles while another continues to fight. One patient may enjoy his role of inadequacy. Muncie says:

The state of the physical health from birth on is important for (1) its effect on the development of the cognitive, conative, and emotional assets; and (2) its effect on the development within the patient of an attitude to the health issue, personal or in others.[65]

A second problem among convalescents has to do with

---

[65] Wendell Muncie, M.D., *Psychobiology and Psychiatry, A Textbook of Normal and Abnormal Human Behavior,* second edition (St. Louis: The C. V. Mosby Company, 1948), p. 102.

isolation and sensitivity. The patient who has passed through an acute illness receives less attention as his condition improves. During this time, he may be overcome with a sense of isolation. Physically, he is still dependent upon others for his care, while mentally he is anxious to resume his former role in life, and emotionally he is sensitive and easily hurt. Groves likens this period of illness to the adolescent stage in the growth of the individual.

The patient is not ill enough to be able to accept without compunction the childlike dependency which his physical weakness makes necessary. Yet if he is no longer suffering pain he is likely to want more attention than is necessary, and may feel that he is being neglected if he happens to find himself alone when he awakens.[66]

Another common problem of convalescence is loneliness. Cabot and Dicks describe loneliness as something that "comes stalking upon us when we are ill because there are so many long, idle hours in which to brood." [67]

Closely connected with loneliness is the problem of boredom, which the convalescent has to face. This is probably worse among men than women, since men tend naturally to be more restless indoors. According to Cabot and Dicks,

Boredom is quite different from acute physical suffering and from other forms of mental suffering, though it may accompany them. It is the internal gnawing of a hungry mind which finds no food to munch. The bored patient can neither stop his mind nor fasten it on any interest. Hence, he preys upon himself like an empty stomach.[68]

In certain types of chronic illness the problem of pain may be paramount. Groves has stated his belief that:

---

[66] Ernest R. Groves and Catherine Groves, *Dynamic Mental Hygiene* (New York: Stackpole and Heck, 1948), p. 102.

[67] Cabot and Dicks, *op. cit.*, p. 60.

[68] *Ibid.*, p. 83.

A man's philosophy of life is never more thoroughly tested than when he faces a future in which he can expect only an increased amount of pain and crippling, as in certain cases of arthritis and other such conditions.[69]

Some patients during convalescence face the problem of solving the far-reaching personality derangements that follow the loss of a limb, or function, or capacity. The amputee, deprived of his feet, faces a small world confined to the chair or bed which he occupies. Many times the newly disabled person lacks the courage to make the effort of attempting a comeback.

A very realistic problem of convalescence may be the fear of dependency, or the economic problem foremost in the minds of most sick persons.

Such consideration not only may keep a person from seeking medical attention as soon as he should, and cause him to try to return to his usual routine before it is wise to do so, but may be the biggest factor in keeping the patient in a state of strain which impedes his recovery. A lasting sense of guilt may be left with the person who sees the whole household suffering because of the economic stress brought on by the expense of his illness.[70]

Finally marital difficulties may arise as the result of convalescence. I have dealt with this problem on several occasions in patients who have had several hospital admissions because of chronic illness. This problem has been well described by Groves:

Since the factors which lead the human being to want sexual union with a particular person are deep-seated and go back to early childhood influences, it can be seen that the changes which a chronic illness can bring about in an individual could block the impulse in the mate.[71]

---

[69] Groves and Groves, *op. cit.*, p. 72.
[70] *Ibid.*, pp. 70–71.
[71] *Ibid.*, p. 74.

The pastor may need to help convince the individual that some other attitude would be more productive of happiness and efficiency, and that cultivating such an attitude will be worth all the effort expended. He can give this help by providing a warm emotional and spiritual atmosphere combined with firm guidance, in order that the individual's hidden assets may be brought forth to take root and grow. The pastor should always remember that:

The potential attitude to illness and handicap can often not be accurately gauged because the subject has never been brought to test on that score. Allowance must be made therefore for the possibility of change in appropriate circumstances in what appear to be permanent attitudes.[72]

In ministering to convalescents, therefore, the pastor should first of all possess the confidence that in this area true miracles do occur. Even the most devastating affliction has yielded to reconditioning when the victim and those around him went at the task with assurance and with the determination to put everything they had into the conquest. It seems appropriate here to refer to one such miracle of science and faith.

Fred Tucholsky had been, prior to November 20, 1930, a happy, active boy, with an ambition to become an athlete. On that date, however, a railway accident cost the thirteen-year-old boy his legs. Most people, seeing him in the succeeding months maimed and helpless on his hospital cot, mentally assigned him to a life of wheel-chair locomotion. With encouragement and a wellspring of determination, however, he rose above his disablement. After many stumbles and falls, he not only became ambulatory with his artificial legs, but learned to swim, to drive an automobile, and to bowl. He can walk up and down stairs and inclines without difficulty. Today, in his thirties, he is the proud

---

[72] Muncie, *op. cit.*, pp. 102–103.

father of two normal, rollicking boys. Fred is a successful office clerk, doing a full day's work and asking no help or quarter from anybody. Here is a convincing demonstration that the age of miracles, far from being past, is perhaps only just beginning.[73]

Second, the pastor should realize that a strong faith in self and in God brings salvation to the convalescent patient. Spiritual faith often suffers enormous strain when physical strength and agility have been rudely cut off, and it is not uncommon for the sufferer to cry out against God in his agony of soul. Previous values and perspectives become distorted; disillusionment settles down; and then it is that society is wrong, the world is wrong, and God is wrong. The poor victim, in his desperate state of mind, finds it difficult to believe that only he, himself, has been changed by his hard experience. Into this experience the pastor should seek to enter, giving off a subtle contagious faith and assurance, which by a sort of spiritual osmosis permeates the depleted spiritual channels of the crippled, the disabled, and the physically circumscribed.

The ministry of sympathy also has its place with the convalescent patient, but it should be a sympathy that calls for action. The giving of sympathy probably requires more skill than any other phase of the pastor's ministry. There is no place for the sentimental, shallow sympathy that weakens the recipient, but there is a place for the kind of sympathy that sets men on their feet and compels them to action. We must realize that tender, loving care is often quite frustrating to the patient, that compassionate ministrations frequently create in him a feeling of helplessness and dependency. One has only to minister to one hypochondriac patient to realize what a fine line of distinction there is between helping and hurting an individ-

---

[73] Cited by Averill and Kempf, *op. cit.*, p. 398.

ual through the giving of sympathy. The disabled must be taught to accept and then to ignore their deficiencies.

Another ministry to the convalescent which should not be overlooked by the pastor could be called occupational therapy. This is especially helpful to the lonely and bored patient. Through what is learned about the patient from conversation, the pastor may be able to suggest something for the individual to do that will occupy his time. For example, the pastor may have a batch of mail that needs to be folded, sealed, and stamped. Requesting the help of an invalid on such a job would be rendering a service to the individual.

Humor can also be used to advantage in the pastor's ministry to convalescent patients. One needs to be able to sense the appropriate time and circumstances for a joke, for a good laugh can often mean much to certain lonely or bored individuals. Cabot and Dicks value humor highly as a tool in the sickroom: "We believe that it is as much a clergyman's duty to train his sense of humor as it is to train his voice." [74]

The pastor will probably make more use of literature with convalescent patients than in any other of his ministries in the general hospital. Various types of literature can be used, including the devotional type, the informational type, literature chosen for specific therapeutic reasons, and literature chosen for its sheer beauty, humor, or interest. Reading is a godsend during the long hours of convalescence.

Finally, it should be noted that the period of convalescence offers the ideal time for an extended counseling ministry to the patient. Every type of problem that arises in the human race will confront the pastor in this ministry. With only a white ceiling overhead and blank walls around

---

[74] Cabot and Dicks, *op. cit.*, p. 66.

him in a hospital room, the patient has nothing to do but think. Over and over again, the chaplain hears the statement—often immediately upon entering the room—"I was just lying here thinking." It is a rare privilege to be allowed to walk around in the innermost chambers of a human mind and witness the intimate struggles of a human soul. Therefore, the pastor should guard these secrets that come to his ears and remember always that, but for the grace of God, he would be the man on the sickbed.

Ministering to the Dying

It is a moving experience to stand and see a person die. The average man or woman usually shrinks from any association with the dying. Yet those who are often in the presence of death learn that it need not be depressing but may be made beautiful by the way in which the dying person and those around him face it. Not only should the pastor consider it an honor to participate in the last moments of an individual's life, but he should also regard it as a sacred opportunity. Attendance at a death is without doubt the most difficult of pastoral ministries, but any shirking of responsibility is bound to leave one with a sense of guilt.

It would be impossible to describe death because its approach may be manifested in many different ways. It is well, however, for the pastor to know certain simple facts concerning the signs of approaching death. Occasionally, I have been in the room of a dying individual and have had the responsibility of summoning the nurse and doctor. The signs of death have been described by Harmer and Henderson as follows:

In sudden death there is obviously no time for the failing circulation to bring about those changes in the appearance and behavior that occur when death comes at the end of an illness. Certain signs do serve, however, as indications that life is approaching its end. First, there is a general slowing of the circulation shown by the fact that the feet, especially, and later the hands, ears, and nose are cold to the touch. Usually, there is excessive sweating; the skin may be pale or mottled from the congestion of blood in the veins. Because the muscles are losing their tone, the body assumes a supine position that requires no support; the jaw sags while the dying man breathes through his mouth, with the flaccid lips and cheeks sucked in and blown outward with each respiration; the reflexes gradually disappear; the pupils fail to react to light; there is inability to swallow.[75]

Some dying persons become semiconscious, disoriented, or delirious. The last condition is especially hard on the family, particularly when the patient uses profane and obscene language.

Some people die mentally many times before they die physically. As Dunbar says,

That is even more true of many sick people as compared with the healthy. These victims of disease, not necessarily through fear, prospect in the valley of death for a long time before they need to take up permanent residence, and they hasten that moment accordingly.[76]

Rollo May has suggested that it is difficult to distinguish normal from neurotic elements in anxiety connected with death, since a normal recognition of death as an objective fact has been so widely repressed in our culture. He advises that, "as a practical measure in clinical work, it may be that, whenever concern about death arises, it is best to work first on the assumption that neurotic elements may be present and to endeavor to ferret them out." [77]

The pastor faces this problem of anxiety about death

[75] Harmer and Henderson, op. cit., pp. 411–12.

[76] Flanders Dunbar, M.D., Mind and Body: Psychosomatic Medicine (New York: Random House, 1947), p. 212.

[77] Rollo May, The Meaning of Anxiety (New York: The Ronald Press Company, 1950), pp. 195–96.

most often in the individual with a malignant disease, who has a waiting period but is fully conscious that death is inevitably near.

One may expect the person facing certain death to react in one of three ways: to accept the fact quietly, to become restless and impatient, or to become very fearful. During a period of conscious waiting for inevitable death in the early future, patients seem to follow a fairly common behavior pattern, although there would certainly be exceptions. Fairbanks has described the steps in this course of behavior as "(1) the desire for additional information; (2) the tendency to reject the fact that one is going to die soon; (3) increased interest in friends and relatives; (4) and, the arranging of business affairs." [78]

Every pastor has to face the question and make a decision as to whether or not death should be discussed with a patient when the doctors say he is not going to live. Some ministers maintain that to discuss death with the patient would be to admit a lack of faith, while others insist that it is a pastoral duty to prepare the individual for meeting God. I have observed that most patients sense that death is near and believe therefore that the entire initiative should be left to the patient. When the question is brought up, the pastor should not avoid dealing with it but should certainly offer any ray of hope for life that can be mentioned. Many times the question will be discussed in detail when both the pastor and the patient are fully aware of the subject, but neither will ever actually use the word "death" itself. If the individual wants it this way, one has no right to violate his desire.

The question of what to tell the patient is even more intense when death is not imminent. Some of the doctors object strongly to telling a patient that his recovery is im-

---

[78] Rollin J. Fairbanks, "Ministering to the Dying," *The Journal of Pastoral Care,* 2:9:3, (Fall) 1948.

possible, while others believe the patient should be told. Still others maintain that patients never really want to know, even though they may ask.

Russell Dicks has recently published an article, based upon a questionnaire sent to doctors entitled, "How Doctors Treat the Dying." Two of the questions and their answers that are particularly relevant to this discussion are quoted as follows:

(1) Do you think a person facing death should be told what he is facing if he asks? Two hundred and seventy-five, or 59.8 percent, answered "yes"; 76, or 16.5 percent, "no"; 65, or 14.1 percent, "depends on patient"; 38, or 8.3 percent, "usually"; and 6, or 1.3 percent, unclassified.

(2) If he does not ask? Fifty-six, or 11.9 percent, said "yes"; 265, or 56.4 percent, "no"; 121 or 25.8 percent, "if necessary for his affairs"; 1, or 0.2 percent, "only if his soul is at stake"; 27, or 5.7 percent, unclassified.[79]

The pastor does not make the diagnosis or determine the prognosis of a patient. It is, therefore, the opinion of this writer that the pastor should stand by and, in consultation with the doctor, render whatever service is possible in view of the policy of the doctor in charge, leaving the answers to medical authority. However, the emotional stability of the patient should probably determine to a large extent what he is told.

Dean Willard L. Sperry, of the Harvard Divinity School, says in this connection:

My own long observation, and thus my matured opinion on the matter are as follows: Whether a doctor is to tell the truth to the patient depends primarily upon his knowledge of the patient and his observation of the patient's own frame of mind. Many very sick persons may suspect that they are going to die; but would rather not be told so in so many words.

[79] Russell L. Dicks, "How Doctors Treat the Dying," reprinted from *The Pastor*, November, 1951.

They prefer to get along without that spoken verdict on their condition. Surely, it is an act of gratuitous unkindness to force the prognosis on such a person.[80]

Some suggestions for the pastor in ministering to the dying are:

(1) Possess a strong religious confidence in God's loving and forgiving spirit, as revealed by Jesus.

(2) Make contact with the patient before a crisis is reached in order that a larger service may be rendered.

(3) Make short, frequent visits, as the dying person often gets lonely.

(4) Avoid showing signs of grief, and help the family to do the same.

(5) Let the patient take the lead in discussion of religious matters. The pastor's role will elicit a reaction of some sort when the minister offers his service. Difficulties will occasionally arise in this connection, since the family sometimes expects the pastor to obtain in five minutes a decision that they have not secured in a lifetime.

(6) Be alert for any signs on the part of the individual that indicate a desire to confess secret sins. The patient may, without making an oral request, show that he would like to talk to the pastor alone. If so, do not hesitate to ask those present to leave the room.

(7) Dicks says, "With a patient who has regrets at going or who is fearful of going, one may use directed listening and quietness. A desire for any direct ministrations about death should come from the patient." [81]

(8) Do not whisper inside or outside the room. The apparent loss of consciousness is not always real.

Since most of the patients who are critically ill or dying

---

[80] Willard L. Sperry, *The Ethical Basis of Medical Practice*. (New York: Paul B. Hoeber, Inc., Medical Book Department of Harper and Brothers, 1950), p. 120.

[81] Cabot and Dicks, *op. cit.*, p. 306.

are unconscious, delirious, under heavy sedation, or just too sick to care, the pastor will probably perform his most fruitful ministry in connection with the family of the dying person. In fact it may be too late to help the patient, but usually the family can be helped a great deal.

Ministering to the Bereaved

Closely related to the pastor's ministry to the dying is his ministry to the bereaved. A knowledge of the emotional reactions at work in a time of bereavement is essential to the work of the pastor. Whether the pastor is aware of it or not, he is in contact with persons suffering bereavement of one kind or another almost every day.

Bereavement is the result of deprivation or separation and is therefore not limited to times of death. The man who has lost his property, the jilted lover, the person who has lost a job or social status, the mother whose "home boy" has joined the army, the amputee, and the divorcee —all are bereaved. Death, because of its finality, is usually thought of as the most serious form of bereavement; hence, this discussion will be concerned chiefly with bereavement caused by death, although the same principles would apply in other situations.

Since Freud's original study of "Mourning and Melancholia," reactions of grief resulting from bereavement have been studied intensively.[82] The one persistent idea present in all these studies seems to be the one implied by Freud, and later formulated by Deutsch: that the "work" of grief must be visualized in the light of the psychoanalytic theory of libido. This theory is set forth in the analogy between the "conservation" of libido on the one hand, and the law of conservation of energy on the other.[83]

---

[82] Sigmund Freud, "Mourning and Melancholia," *Collected Papers* IV, 10:152.

[83] Helene Deutsch, "Absence of Grief," *Psychoanalytic Quarterly*, 6:12, 1937.

More recently, Erich Lindemann made an extensive and systematic study of grief reactions from the psychiatric point of view. This report divides grief reactions into two classes: normal and morbid.[84]

In normal grief reactions there are marked physical evidences of distress such as sighing respiration, tightness in the throat, shortness of breath, a feeling of emptiness in the abdomen, and a feeling of exhaustion. The respiratory disturbance is most conspicuous when the patient is made to discuss his grief.

The patient's sensory perception generally is somewhat altered. This alteration is suggested by the complaint that things seem to be unreal, by the increased emotion distance from people, and by preoccupation with the image of the deceased.

Another symptom of grief is the tendency toward preoccupation with guilt feelings. "If we had only brought him to the hospital earlier," is the remark most often heard by the pastor. Bereaved persons accuse themselves violently for the least omission relative to the deceased. They seem to feel that blame for the loss must be borne by someone.

There is a disconcerting loss of warmth in relationships to other people, evidenced by irritability and anger, or by a wish not to be bothered by others at a time when friends and relatives make a special effort to keep up friendly relationships. This hostility may be directed at some person actually or presumably involved with the loved one's death. This person may be the physician or some member of the family.

Another symptom may be the loss of patterns of conduct, demonstrated by "pushing" of speech, restlessness, inability to sit still, aimless movements, and a continual search for something to do. A bereaved individual may have difficulty

---

[84] Erich Lindemann, "Symptomatology and Management of Acute Grief," *American Journal of Psychiatry*, 101:141 (September, 1944).

in such a simple matter as giving the pastor instructions concerning a telephone call.

Finally, a characteristic not so conspicuous as the others is the appearance of traits of the deceased in the behavior of the bereaved. Every hospital chaplain is familiar with a milder form of this symptom, which is expressed in the bereaved person's desire to take up activities left off by the deceased.

Since ministry to the bereaved occupies a central place in the pastor's work, a knowledge of Lindemann's analysis of morbid grief reactions is no less important than an understanding of these normal symptoms. Morbid reactions can be even more baffling, and actual harm can result from an improper handling of them. Seven morbid grief reactions are listed by Lindemann.

First, there is postponed, or delayed, grief reaction. Often the pastor will observe an individual who is apparently calm, with no outward show of grief, immediately after a relative dies. Lindemann indicates that years later the grief reaction may become very evident.

The second symptom of morbid grief reaction involves overactivity without a sense of loss. The bereaved person may even appear to be elated and start engaging in activities out of all proportion to his normal behavior.

A third distorted reaction has to do with the acquisition of symptoms associated with the last illness of the deceased. For example, a member of the family who nursed the deceased may go to bed immediately after the funeral, complaining of the same symptoms with which the individual died.

Fourth, psychosomatic complaints may develop in the person suffering from distorted grief reaction. Lindemann mentions rheumatoid arthritis, asthma, and ulcerative colitis as predominant examples. I recall talking to a young man who, shortly after the death of his mother, came into the hospital suffering with ulcerative colitis.

The fifth symptom is a conspicuous alteration in the relationship to friends and relatives. Progressive isolation follows this irritability and withdrawal from social contacts. While hostility appears to be spread out over all relationships, it may also be directed furiously against specific persons.

Sixth, some persons succeed in repressing their hostility; they become wooden and formal, with affectivity resembling schizophrenic patterns. Closely related to this reaction is a lasting loss of patterns of social interaction. The individual might lose all initiative or begin the excessive use of alcohol.

Finally, the distorted grief reaction may take the form of agitated depression with tension, agitation, insomnia, feelings of worthlessness, bitter self-accusation, and an obvious need for punishment.

Lindemann concludes his analysis of grief with some suggestions as to its proper management. First of all, he recognizes the measures of religion, dogma, divine grace, and rituals, which maintain the patient's interaction with others. Comfort alone, however, does not provide adequate assistance in grief work. The bereaved must accept the pain of the bereavement, review his relationships with the deceased, and become acquainted with the alterations in his own modes of emotional reaction. His fear of insanity and of accepting the surprising changes in his feelings, especially the overflow of hostility, has to be worked through. It is necessary for the bereaved to express his sorrow and sense of loss and to find an acceptable formulation of his future relationship to the deceased. Finally, the bereaved will have to verbalize his feelings of guilt and will have to find persons around him whom he can use as "primers" for the acquisition of new patterns of conduct.

Another study of grief reactions in later life adds:

Grief reactions in later life have been studied in twenty-five subjects, twenty-three of whom attended an old-age counseling service. The most striking features in this group were: a relative paucity of overt grief and of conscious guilt feelings, a preponderance of somatic illness precipitated or accentuated by the bereavement, a tendency to extreme exaggeration of the common idealization of the deceased with a blotting-out of all "dark" features; a tendency to self-isolation and to hostility against some living person.[85]

The point to be especially noted in these findings is that the *older* person is often ready to "channel" into somatic illness material that would produce overt emotional conflict.

It is in order now to relate these studies of grief reactions specifically to the work of the pastor. It should always be kept in mind that one's ministry to the bereaved family is strengthened by any previous relationships. Furthermore, it should be emphasized that the pastor occupies one of the most strategic positions in society for helping bereaved families get started into a healthy state of bereavement and thus avoid later morbid reactions. His services are especially valuable in the case of individuals who are blaming themselves for the death of the deceased. The two following examples will serve to illustrate this statement.

A father was holding his fourteen-month-old son on his lap, feeding him his evening meal, when suddenly the baby jumped and started falling to the floor. The father caught the child before he struck the floor, but in the process a blood vessel ruptured in the baby's head. The child was placed in the hospital and died the next morning.

This father was in mental anguish, blaming himself for

---

[85] Karl Stern, M.D., Gwendolyn M. Williams, B.D., and Miguel Prados, M.D., "Grief Reactions in Later Life," *The American Journal of Psychiatry,* 108:293:4, (October) 1951.

carelessness. I spent an hour with this man and his wife and listened to the father pour out his feelings. The man showed a definite change of countenance when, after I had reassured him that it was one of those accidents which could happen to anybody, the wife spoke up and said, "What he is saying is true. I do not hold you responsible for it." So constructively did this couple make their adjustment to their tragic experience of bereavement that twelve months later I had the privilege of assisting them in adopting a child.

On another occasion, a young man who was considered the "black sheep" in his family got into trouble and wired his aged father to come to his rescue. The father traveled a long distance by train and, immediately upon arriving on the scene, had a heart attack. He was brought into the hospital, where he died shortly afterward. The son's first remark to the chaplain as he stood by the bed of his father, was, "I killed my father, just as sure as if I had shot him." His next remark was, "Chaplain, you have got to help me." I invited the young man to my office and listened as he paced the floor and related his life story. This individual was never heard from again, but it is believed that enough was accomplished in the beginning stages of his bereavement process to prevent later morbid grief reactions.

Obviously, cases of this extreme nature do not happen every day in the hospital, but in all bereaved persons a tendency toward self-blame is present to a greater or lesser degree. This self-blame may be based on real guilt, or on purely imaginary sins of omission or commission.

I was shocked on one occasion to see a man jump completely over the top of a hospital bed and land on his head and shoulders on the other side, continuing to roll on the floor until picked up bodily and put in a chair. This happened when his fourteen-year-old daughter died. When I remarked to the surgeon that it was hard to understand such a severe reaction, the surgeon replied, "If you had examined the girl, you would understand. Her sexual development was equal to that of an adult. The father had probably been fondling her for a long time." The emotional shock which this man received would be just as likely, in another case, to produce an appearance of complete apathy.

More specifically, just how does the pastor deal with the ordinary problems of bereavement that arise day by day in the hospital setting?

1. After the doctor and nurse have finished with the bereaved family, the pastor should invite them to a quiet place. In this way the doctor and nurse will be relieved, other patients will not be disturbed, and the pastor can minister to the family during the short waiting period before they leave the hospital. At this time any small service which is necessary, such as a telephone call, can be rendered.

2. In many cases the pastor needs to remember the advice of Cabot and Dicks:

Unless one has been much with the family during the latter days of the illness one does not realize how tired they are, how much on edge their nerves are, and how much they need rest. Relief from the strain of seeing a loved person suffer is often their dominant feeling. Loss of sleep and the strain of mingled hope and fear leave many so exhausted that they are almost numb emotionally and reproach themselves because the sense of relief overshadows grief. They need to be assured that this is normal and right, that they have nothing to reproach themselves for.[86]

3. Above all things to be avoided is the giving of cheap, superficial consolation. It should be kept in mind that the pastor helps more by what he stands for than by what he says. The minister represents to the bereaved all the values of religious faith, such as forgiveness, immortality, hope,

---

[86] Cabot and Dicks, *op. cit.*, p. 315.

the goodness of God, and the love of God toward every individual. To remember this is to avoid trite statements such as, "He is better off. He would not like for you to grieve this way. Later you will feel better. You have lost, but he has gained. God has a purpose in it this way." It is definitely in order, however, to express one's sympathy. This should be done in a simple, down-to-earth statement or conveyed by a squeeze of the hand, pressure on the arm, or other signs that are just as meaningful. Sometimes the family may be consoled by the pastor's statement of his belief (when it is sincere) that they did all in their power for the loved one, by obtaining the best that medical science had to offer.

4. The first need which the bereaved has is for support from others. As Rogers has said,

Often the minister is acceptable to the bereaved when another is not, because he is already known as one whom he can trust, and to whom hurt feelings and sore spirits can be made known. In strong grief there may be a tendency for the bereaved to withdraw at the very time when he needs support. The ability of the minister to make contact with him may be the factor which keeps him from isolation, and hence becomes his chief support.[87]

5. The pastor should pass on to the bereaved any parts of conversations which he had with the patient that might be comforting. Oftentimes, the individual facing death will tell the minister that everything is all right in his relationship with God. Words of this nature can mean a great deal to the family. In fact, the pastor will sometimes be asked the question, "Did he talk to you about how it was with his soul?"

6. The pastor should pray with the family when the relationship indicates that prayer would be appropriate. The

---

[87] William F. Rogers, "Needs of the Bereaved," *Pastoral Psychology*, 1:5:18, (June) 1950.

prayer should not be too lengthy, but should state simply the course of a normal grief reaction which keeps the individual close to reality, and then should invoke God's divine Spirit to undergird and support the bereaved during the experience. Along with prayer, there is the accumulated wisdom of Scriptures and poetry that can assert conviction in the situation.

7. Carroll Wise warns against structuralizing grief in religious ideas:

> Persons with intense grief reactions will often seek to bolster their negative feelings in religious ideas. On the other hand, the approach of the pastor may encourage this in a person who otherwise would work through the grief process in a normal way. One illustration of this is seen in the mother who spent years thinking about her dead son being "up in heaven." The more she thought about the son being "up in heaven" the more she suffered because he was not here on earth. . . . Premature urging of the idea of immortality may retard the emotional readjustment to bereavement.[88]

8. The pastor should help the individual to accept the pain of bereavement. If the feeling of loss is repressed and denied expression, it tends to engender morbid grief reactions and may become manifest later in some disguised form such as behavior difficulty, malfunction of the physical organism, or neurotic tendencies. Men, especially, try to avoid showing emotion, as some think it is a sign of weakness. The pastor should encourage the expression of grief where there are signs that the individual is fighting against it. This encouragement can be given through such a gentle suggestion as, "Go ahead and cry. I would do the same, if I were in your place." An outward expression of sorrow and of the sense of loss helps the bereaved to adjust to the shock of breaking off the personal relationship or

---

[88] Carroll A. Wise, *Pastoral Counseling, Its Theory and Practice* (New York: Harper and Brothers, 1951), p. 215.

sphere of interaction and to gain emancipation from the deceased.

The suggestions made thus far can be used by the pastor during the brief period of contact with the family immediately following the death of a loved one. Joshua Loth Liebman's three laws for governing grief serve as something of a summary:

(1) Express as much grief as you actually feel.

(2) We must learn how to extricate ourselves from the bondage of the physical existence and coexistence of the loved one.

(3) When death destroys an important relationship, it is essential that someone be found partially capable of replacing that relationship.[89]

Liebman's third rule should be kept in mind during extended counseling with an individual relative to bereavement. Occasionally a doctor will request the pastor to tell a patient that a member of his family has died since he came to the hospital. This situation leads to extended counseling which involves all the suggestions made by Lindemann at the beginning of this discussion, except those concerning the extreme types of morbid reactions. Even in these cases the pastor should work with the psychiatrist.

As was indicated in the beginning, bereavement is not limited to death only, and often the pastor has an opportunity to spend considerable time with a bereaved individual who is a patient in the hospital. For the sake of emphasis, it should be stated that relationships with bereaved persons arise much more often than the average person would realize. Patients often are admitted to the hospital shortly after passing through a bereavement crisis. Many times the pastor will discover, in talking to a recently

---

[89] Joshua Loth Liebman, *Peace of Mind* (New York: Simon and Schuster, 1946), pp. 113–15.

admitted patient, that the person has not adequately worked through a bereavement that took place some years previously. Amputations are frequent occurrences in a general hospital, and the loss of a limb is almost always followed by depression and a bereavement crisis. Many of the suggestions already offered would apply equally in cases where extended counseling can be given, and several others may also be presented briefly:

1. Through directed listening, help the individual who is having a delayed grief reaction to see the relationship between the earlier bereavement situation and the present difficulty. Here, skill in counseling is essential and the work should be done in co-operation with the physician or psychiatrist.

2. Help the individual to express verbally his feelings of hostility and guilt. As Rogers has pointed out:

In any relationship there is a strong likelihood of the development of hostile feelings. . . . These feelings may have been expressed as they arose, but more often they are partially if not wholly suppressed, especially with a parent or a spouse, where it is considered wrong to express or even to feel hostility. . . . To clear the way for the doing of grief work, hostile feelings must be expressed.[90]

3. Aid the bereaved to find new meaning in life and to rework his philosophy in relation to the catastrophe that has come to him. This help can be given after the bereaved does the grief work, but not before. After reliving the experience and expressing sorrow and loss, guilt and hostility, the bereaved can think in terms of immortality and can be made to realize that death is as natural as birth and that the Holy Spirit is sufficient to meet his needs.

My experience as a hospital chaplain has caused me to believe that one of the most frequent emotional problems

---

[90] Rogers, *op. cit.*, p. 19.

encountered by the pastor is that of bereavement. Oftentimes the symptoms of bereavement are overlooked or not recognized as such, and the minister fails to supply the help which he alone can give to a bereaved person. The following are a few of the situations in which the pastor might watch for symptoms suggesting that the bereavement process is at work:

1. When there is a divorce or separation, one or both of the parties may suffer severe grief.

2. After a son or husband enters the army or goes overseas, the mother or wife may react more violently than the average person.

3. When the last child goes away to college or gets married, the reaction of the parents sometimes exceeds that of mere homesickness.

4. Individuals who have suffered a sudden loss of property many times experience grief reactions.

5. The individual who retires from a lifetime job should be observed closely by the pastor for signs of depression.

6. The necessity for placing a feeble-minded child in an institution can create a bereavement situation for a family.

7. When a limb is amputated, almost invariably the patient feels a sense of bereavement for the lost member of the body. This is particularly true of a woman who has a breast removed, since she feels that a part of her womanhood is lost.

8. Children may experience bereavement situations which seem trivial to adults. The child who has moved from one community to another or has lost a pet or toy to which he had become closely attached needs more understanding than he receives in many instances. Children often feel bereaved when they are forbidden to associate with playmates from "the wrong side of the tracks" to whom they have become attached, or when their parents leave them in the care of others for a considerable length of time

while they take a vacation. Separation from those who he is most dependent upon is interpreted as rejection b the small child and creates a bereavement situation.

The alert pastor can do much to help parents recognize and understand grief reactions in their children. The one rule to be remembered above all is that the small child should not be sent away from home when there is a death in the family.

APPENDIX A

These recommendations were adopted by the Southern Baptist Hospital Chaplains' and Administrators' Convention held in Chicago in February, 1953. They are presented verbatim and were adopted to be used as a guide for future reference in selection and appointment of chaplains in Southern Baptist Hospitals.

Recommendations for the Southern Baptist Hospital Chaplaincy

The renewed emphasis placed by the medical profession on the concept of health as "wholeness" of life, the emphasis placed upon the vital relationship between one's way of life and his health, and the strategic place of healing as a means of evangelizing, make it imperative that we consider some recommendations for the Baptist Hospital Chaplaincy and suggest basic qualifications for this type of ministry.

It is therefore the intention of the Committee on Hospital Chaplaincy of the Southwide Baptist Hospital Association to recommend the minimum training experience necessary for a minister seeking appointment as a full-time chaplain in our hospitals and to describe goals and practices normally expected of him. This statement is prepared for hospital administrators, boards of directors, medical staffs, and church authorities who are charged with the responsibility of selecting chaplains and who desire a high quality of religious ministry within their hospitals and who wish to strengthen and improve their chaplaincy service.

A. *Formal Qualifications of the Chaplain*

The minister seeking appointment as a chaplain is expected to meet these minimum basic qualifications:

1. Ordination as a minister and appropriate denominational endorsement and evidence of current approval within the denomination.

2. College and seminary degrees.

3. Six months of specialized training in a qualified chaplains' training center and written recommendation by the director of the center attended. This training to have been obtained in a general hospital with psychiatric service or a general hospital and psychiatric hospital.

4. That he shall not have been inactive in the ministry for a period of more than one year at the time of appointment.

B. *Personal Qualifications of the Chaplain*

1. Probably the most important quality of the chaplain is his temperament—"that more or less stable affective pattern characteristic of an individual." His effectiveness in pastoral care and counseling is measured by his ability to relate easily to people and to produce a calm, relaxed and worshipful atmosphere in the sickroom.

2. The health of the chaplain is a matter of supreme importance. The heavy schedule of activities both within and without the hospital setting, as well as the emotional and mental strain of his work demand vigorous physical and emotional health. In addition to this is his constant risk of contagion of diseases.

3. The marital status of the chaplain has a direct bearing on his ministry in the hospital environment since

two of his most important responsibilities include pastoral relationship to student nurses and marital counseling with patients having domestic problems.

4. The social background and cultural pattern in which the chaplain was reared is likewise very important because of their direct effect upon personal counseling. A lack of understanding of the religious background of a person may cause the chaplain to fail to recognize the appropriateness of prayer in several situations and thereby lose his usefulness to these people.

5. Another very important qualification in the choice of a person to provide a religious ministry among the physically ill is the type of evangelistic training he has had. Hospitals are among the most useful instruments for home mission work which the denomination possesses. It is imperative that the chaplain know the nature of the hospital environment and familiarize himself with the nature of illnesses, drugs, or treatments in use in the sickroom as well as the religious background of the patients. The chaplain should be primarily interested that the patient be made whole in body, mind, and spirit so that he may live the abundant life.

6. Although the age of the chaplain is of relative importance, it is particularly desirable at this stage of development in the field of religion as related to health that more young ministers dedicate themselves to the hospital chaplaincy, since these institutions offer the most fruitful fields for research in the relationship between religion and health.

C. *The Appointment of the Chaplain*

1. The appointment of the chaplain should be officially handled like all other hospital appointments by the administrator of the hospital with the approval and support of the Board of Trustees. He should be responsible, as any other department head, to the administrator, but

also to the Religious Activities Committee of the Board of Trustees when such a committee exists.

A committee made up of denominational representatives outside of the Board of Trustees is not likely to be as well acquainted with the needs and nature of the hospital ministry, and would be subject to pressures and "pulls" that often arise in connection with such an appointment for a place of retirement or a political stepping stone. On the other hand, the advantage of having a committee from the Board of Trustees, including ministers to work with the administrator in selecting a chaplain lies in the fact that the administrator would have help from other professional men in judging the qualifications of candidates of a like profession.

2. *The Salary of the Chaplain*

For the sake of harmony within the hospital the chaplain, as any other department head, should be paid by the hospital and not sponsored by some church or association of churches to whom he would be obligated for his ministry rather than to the hospital. His salary should be comparable to that of men of similar training in the church pastorate. In addition to salary, the hospital should provide for his attendance at the vital meetings of the denomination such as the Chaplains' Association and State and Southern Baptist Convention.

3. *The Chaplain's Quarters*

The chaplain should have a private office where he may engage in his pastoral functions of counseling with either hospital personnel or with a patient referred by a doctor, or where he may take the bereaved family from the room of the deceased. This office should be as conveniently located for easy access by pastors from without as well as by persons within the hospital. It should be equipped for maximum effectiveness.

Since the chaplain, like the resident doctor in the

hospital, is subject to call by a doctor or nurse at any time of day or night, it is a decided advantage to live near the hospital so that he is easily accessible in case of emergencies.

D. *Worship in the Hospital*

All scheduled religious services should be either led by the chaplain or arranged through him. Young people's societies and missionary groups should only be brought into the hospital under careful supervision and for the purpose of making a recognized contribution to the patient's welfare. Ordained ministers, commissioned workers, and qualified and responsible visitors should be permitted to call upon patients of their acquaintance, but indiscriminate visiting on the part of anyone should be discouraged. No outside religious worker should be permitted to pass out literature without the chaplain's permission.

An important part of the chaplain's equipment to provide worship in the hospital environment is a good intercommunication system to each bed, although the worshipful atmosphere created by the chaplain's visit at the bedside cannot be replaced.

Every hospital chaplain faces the difficult task of how to spend his time wisely. Certainly the chaplain will spend most of his time with those patients under severe and mental stress, or who especially need spiritual resources.

With several hundred beds the problem of finding these persons in need is intensified.

The chaplain "finds" those who need his services in the following manner:

1. The physician asks the chaplain to call on his patient. These are usually persons with definite and acute needs and should be seen without fail.

2. A nurse, social worker or other hospital employee asks the chaplain to call on the patient.

3. A relative asks the chaplain to call on the patient.

4. The patient's pastor asks the chaplain to call.

5. The patient himself asks the chaplain to call.

6. In addition to his ministry to these patients who have been referred to him, the chaplain usually discovers many who need his care during his morning hours of generalized visiting. Many of these will need to be followed up with more intensive pastoral care at some specified time convenient to both.

Should the ministry of the chaplain not be acceptable to any patient, a minister of the patient's choice should be called in.

Conclusion

The primary purpose of the chaplain in the hospital environment is that of personalizing the vitality of the Christian religion, but at all times he must co-operate to the fullest extent with every other member of the healing team.

Although the chaplain's main function is ministering to the patients and their families, this is not all he contributes to the hospital. While the administrator forms the attitudes and general atmosphere of the hospital, the chaplain can have a definite influence on the morale and well-being of all within.

The trained chaplain inevitably becomes the pastoral counselor for many members of the hospital staff and employees and by all means should be available to all within the hospital community. In addition, he can be useful as counselor for student nurses, advisor on religious activities for the school of nursing and classroom lecturer. As a goodwill ambassador, the chaplain can be valuable to the hospital as a builder of vital public relations, especially in regard to correlating the hospital with the denomination.

As a representative of God, the hospital chaplain through his understanding and poise, word and deed, seeks to encourage one, relieve another of worry, aid a third to bear suffering, break the grip of despair for a fourth, gain serenity for one facing death, and to comfort the bereaved; so that individuals may be led to personal growth, deeper understanding of their fellow men, and increasing consciousness of God.

COMMITTEE ON CHAPLAINCY

APPENDIX B

THE PROGRAM OF CLINICAL PASTORAL TRAINING AVAILABLE THROUGH THE DEPARTMENT OF PASTORAL CARE OF THE NORTH CAROLINA BAPTIST HOSPITAL AND THE BOWMAN GRAY SCHOOL OF MEDICINE

Through its courses in clinical training, the Hospital's Department of Pastoral Care makes available the many facilities of this institution for the scientific study of the role of religion in the treatment of the mentally and physically ill. These courses are offered in the conviction that there are values to be derived from a clinical study of emotional problems which cannot be obtained through a theoretical approach.

Preconceived theories on theology are consequently laid aside as much as possible, and religion is examined as it is lived out in the "human document." The main objective of the course is that of teaching pastoral care through practice in a controlled environment. It actually offers a proving ground for theological training and theoretical studies in pastoral care. The course is built upon the student's face-to-face relationship with the patient, and not upon a lecture method.

Eight-week courses are offered during the summer months. These classes are open to pastors, student secretaries, seminary students, and any other full-time religious workers desiring training in personal counseling. Southeastern Theological Seminary allows four hours credit for these eight weeks toward the B.D. degree.

The tuition fee for the eight weeks is $15.00. The hospital furnishes living quarters and allows the students to eat in the hospital dining hall for 65¢ per meal. The hospital has no facilities for married couples, but rooms can easily be obtained near by.

Each class is limited to a maximum of eight people, and the methods of teaching and the requirements of the course leave the student free to progress as fast as he desires. A two-hour seminar is held each morning from eight until ten o'clock, Monday through Friday, during the eight weeks of the course. The one hundred hours of seminar study are conducted according to the principles of group psychotherapy. The leader attempts at all times to create a "permissive" relationship, in which individual personality reactions may have freedom of response in the atmosphere of the group. The lecture method is used for the first three days only while the students are becoming oriented to the hospital environment.

The five main subjects discussed by the group are: (1) the mechanics of hospital visitation, (2) the art of counseling, (3) personality development, (4) the mind-body relationship, and (5) the application of clinical findings to the pastorate. The discussion of each of these subjects is directly related to a factual case history. The students are assigned parallel reading which corresponds with the general direction of the seminar discussion. Furthermore, during the first week of the course the student chooses a subject for special study and reads all the material that he can find on that subject. To this information he adds a case history of some individual with whom he has worked and whose problem is related to his special interest. This ma-

terial is then presented to the seminar for critical evalua-
tion by the group. The following questions are paramount
in every seminar discussion of a case history: What did
the counselor say that he should not have said? How may
the counselor's statements be improved upon? What is the
heart of the individual's difficulty? What can a minister do
as the situation now stands? What could a minister in the
pastorate have done to prevent the difficulty from arising?
What could the educational program of the church contribute to this individual? How could the preaching ministry affect this person?

Each student is assigned approximately twenty-five beds
in the hospital, and assumes full responsibility as chaplain
of the patients who occupy these beds during the eight-week
period. These beds are scattered all over the hospital, so
that all types of patients who come to the institution may
be represented. During the first three weeks of the course,
each student is required to write a verbatim account of
what was said by himself and the patient during three of
the visits made each day. The students are instructed to
write up brief visits in the beginning, so that they can record every word spoken. At the end of three weeks, each
student is supposed to be working intensively with at least
three patients at all times, and is required to write up,
verbatim, one counseling session a day. These sessions are
begun when the patient enters the hospital, and each visit
with that person during his hospital stay is recorded, so
that an account of the entire pastoral relationship is made
available. All of these verbatim records are examined by
the chaplain in private with the student, and some are
chosen for discussion in the seminar.

The student has access to the chaplain or a psychiatrist
on the medical staff of the hospital if he wishes a better
understanding of his own personality reactions in order to
render a more effective ministry to others. These personal

interviews are not required but are encouraged, because this course is based upon the assumption that one who is to help others must first understand himself.

Various members of the medical staff are invited to lead the seminar from time to time. The department of psychiatry is especially helpful in this connection, and its staff members are called upon frequently.

A winter course designed particularly for pastors is offered each year, beginning on the second Monday in January and running for six weeks. This course follows the same general plan as that described above, but it is less intensive and relies more on the lecture method, since many pastors do not have an adequate reading knowledge in the field of pastoral care. In order that pastors may not have to spend the week end away from their churches, the seminar begins at ten o'clock on Mondays and closes at noon on Fridays.

The hospital also offers *internships* in the field of pastoral care. To be eligible, the applicant must have had at least one summer class of clinical pastoral training or its equivalent. Internship periods may be of three, six, nine, or twelve months' duration, depending upon the desire of the student. The hospital pays $125.00 a month. The intern is furnished a room for $10.00 a month and is allowed to purchase meals in the dining hall for 65¢ per.

The intern has access to all the facilities in the medical center that are related to his work, including classes on the mind-body relationship taught in the medical school, ward conferences led by doctors on the hospital floor, and staff conferences held in a private psychiatric hospital connected with the medical school, as well as supervision by the chaplain of the hospital. He is also given an opportunity to do formal office counseling with people who come in for this purpose from the surrounding community.

Other Baptist hospitals now making their clinical facilities available to the minister are: The New Orleans Baptist Hospital, New Orleans, Louisiana, The Alexandria Baptist Hospital, Alexandria, Louisiana, and, The Memorial Baptist Hospital, Houston, Texas.

BIBLIOGRAPHY

Alexander, Franz, *Psychosomatic Medicine.* New York: W. W. Norton and Company, Inc., 1950. 300 pp.

Blackwood, Andrew W., *Pastoral Work: A Source Book for Ministers.* Philadelphia: The Westminster Press, 1945. 252 pp.

Boisen, Anton T., *The Exploration of the Inner World: A Study of Mental Disorder and Religious Experience.* New York: Willet, Clark and Company, 1936. xi, 392 pp.

Bonnell, John Sutherland, *Pastoral Psychiatry.* New York: Harper and Brothers, 1938. xii, 237 pp.

Cabot, R. C., and Russell L. Dicks, *The Art of Ministering to the Sick.* New York: The Macmillan Company, 1947. viii, 384 pp.

Cannon, Walter B., *The Wisdom of the Body.* New York: W. W. Norton and Company, Inc., 1932. 333 pp.

Dawson, George Gordon, *Healing: Pagan and Christian.* New York: The Macmillan Company, 1935. ix, 322 pp.

Dicks, Russell L., *Pastoral Work and Personal Counseling.* Revised edition. New York: The Macmillan Company, 1949. xii, 195 pp.

Douglas, Lloyd C., *The Minister's Everyday Life.* New York: Charles Scribner's Sons, 1924. xii, 220 pp.

Dunbar, Flanders, *Mind and Body: Psychosomatic Medicine.* New York: Random House, 1947. 263 pp.

Freud, Sigmund, "Mourning and Melancholia," *Collected Papers.* Vols. I–IV. London: Hogarth Press, 1946.

Garlick, Phyllis L., *Health and Healing: A Christian Interpretation.* London: Edinburgh House, 1948. v, 80 pp.

Gladden, Washington, *The Christian Pastor and the Working Church*. New York: Charles Scribner's Sons, 1898. 485 pp.

Gray, George W., *The Advancing Front of Medicine*. New York: McGraw-Hill Book Company, 1941. viii, 425 pp.

Gray, Giles Wilkeson, and Claude Merton Wise, *The Bases of Speech*. New York: Harper and Brothers, 1934. xvii, 439 pp.

Groves, Ernest R., and Catherine Groves, *Dynamic Mental Hygiene*. New York: Stackpole and Heck, 1948. 559 pp.

Harmer, Bertha, and Virginia Henderson, *Textbook of the Principles and Practices of Nursing*, edition 4, revised. New York: The Macmillan Company, 1946.

Harrower, M. R., editor, *Training in Clinical Psychology*. New York: Josiah Macy, Jr. Foundation, 1947.

Hiltner, Seward, *Pastoral Counseling*. New York: Abingdon-Cokesbury Press, 1949. 291 pp.

Holman, Charles T., *The Cure of Souls: A Socio-psychological Approach*. Chicago: The University of Chicago Press, 1932. xv, 331 pp.

Jacobson, Edmund, *Progressive Relaxation*. Chicago: University of Chicago Press, 1929. xvii, 493 pp.

———, *You Must Relax*. New York: McGraw-Hill Press, 1934. xv, 201 pp.

Kemp, Charles F., *Physicians of the Soul: A History of Pastoral Counseling*. New York: The Macmillan Company, 1947. xi, 314 pp.

Kraines, S. H., and E. L. Thetford, *Managing Your Mind*. New York: The Macmillan Company, 1945. viii, 374 pp.

Liebman, Joshua Loth, *Psychiatry and Religion*. Boston: The Beacon Press, 1948. xix, 202 pp.

Mackenzie, J. G., *Souls in the Making*. New York: The Macmillan Company, 1929. 259 pp.

May, Rollo, *The Art of Counseling*. New York: Abingdon-Cokesbury Press, 1939. 247 pp.

———, *The Meaning of Anxiety*. New York: The Ronald Press Company, 1950. xv, 376 pp.

McNeill, John T., *A History of the Cure of Souls*. New York: Harper and Brothers, 1951. xii, 371 pp.